GIVE ME,
GET ME,
BUY ME!

D1509692

GIVE ME, GET ME, BUY ME!

Preventing or Reversing
Entitlement in Your Child's Attitude

DONNA CORWIN

Health Communications, Inc.
Deerfield Beach, Florida

www.hcibooks.com

Library of Congress Cataloging-in-Publication Data

Corwin, Donna G.

Give me, get me, buy me! : preventing or reversing entitlement in your child's
attitude / Donna Corwin.

   p. cm.

   ISBN-13: 978-0-7573-1386-8

   ISBN-10: 0-7573-1386-8

   1. Pampered child syndrome.   2. Entitlement attitudes.   3. Child rearing.
4. Child psychology.   I. Title.

   HQ769.C457 2010

   649'.7—dc22

                             2009053210

Publisher: Health Communications, Inc.
           3201 S.W. 15th Street
           Deerfield Beach, FL 33442–8190

Cover design by Larissa Hise Henoch
Interior design and formatting by Lawna Patterson Oldfield

Alexandra—My precious daughter,
my inspiration, my joy

Stan—My husband, my mentor,
my believer

CONTENTS

ACKNOWLEDGMENTS

Stan Corwin—Thank you for your insightful edits and invaluable comments. You always encourage me and push me forward.

Ann Benya—Eight books and thousands of pages later, you are still the best at making sense of my scribble. Thank you.

Thank you to my friends and associates whose input and perspectives were so valuable in creating this book.

Michele Matrisciani—My editor and cheerleader, who believed in this book from the beginning. Thank you for your support and valuable guidance.

Thanks also to Carol Rosenberg and the editorial staff at HCI Books.

To the parents who openly shared their stories, fears, and feelings.

AUTHOR'S NOTE

It is difficult to talk about entitlement without discussing the problems we have experienced financially as a nation. Lulled into apathy and spending sprees, a large majority of Americans have been seduced by credit cards, high-priced media ads, and Wall Street selling us and subsidizing the idea of the "good life." It wasn't necessarily the message of reaching for the good life that has gotten us into the bind we are in now, but rather the mentality that anyone and everyone is entitled to the good life, never mind if the means are available to pay for it. The message was go ahead—buy and spend freely. We became intoxicated by things. You work hard, so you should reap the rewards by saying yes to your whims; you are entitled to that aren't you? This financial de-empowerment message, whether fabricated or not, has been translated to our children. We spent what we didn't have, forgot to save for a "rainy day," and competed fiercely to have the biggest and the best. The mantra *Give Me, Get Me, Buy Me* was subtly sold to us as parents by a society bent on having it all. Our children watched us hand over credit cards like they were candy. We bought everything they asked for without hesitation and set an example of overindulgence with no financial boundaries.

I fell into this entitlement trap. I raised an entitled child. She is wonderful, free-spirited, curious, intelligent, creative, and "spoiled." When she and her friends are told, "We can't afford that" or "It's too much money," a glazed look comes across their faces. Entitled children are not used to hearing these words. It is difficult to adjust to the real world where there are new financial boundaries.

Having been raised on the heels of the boomer generation, I spent money so freely and gave so easily that a reality check came when the bottom dropped out of the economy. The post–boomers entitlement generation, those born between 1979 and 1994, were the recipients of free-spending parents. Their role models were parents who coveted things in a time when the competition race was at its height. We competed over whose child had the most toys, got the better grades, made the top private schools, had the top sports equipment. Then these post-boomers transferred their entitled attitudes to their children, truly believing the good times and money would never end.

We now have children who are unprepared for fiscal responsibility and have delusions of grandeur when it comes to emphasis on material things. The big house, big car, and big job may temporarily be out of our children's grasp. They are more unaware of the outside world and what it means to save and to sacrifice.

As parents now struggle financially, there is more worry about paying bills than incurring them. Left with unsettling and unpredictable economic scenarios, parents are also left with entitled children, who have attitudes that clash with the money-conservative mindset they are forced to adopt. As hard as this time may be for many parents, in other ways, it is a chance to take hold of values that are really important in order to have a strong family unit in difficult times. This is the bright side we will be focusing on in *Give Me, Get Me, Buy Me,* with information on how to raise a child with a social conscience, who is also a self-sufficient, independent, and capable human being.

INTRODUCTION

Entitled children are created, not born. I became a Give Me, Get Me, Buy Me parent early on. Not wanting to deprive my princess of anything, I indulged her until she started to get used to the good life. In fact, I trained her so well that, like Pavlov's dog, when we entered a shopping mall, she didn't start to salivate or bark, but she did whine incessantly. If I passed a shop without buying her something, passed the food court without getting her a cookie (even before dinner), or didn't run around like a crazy person to find her the same super, strappy, pink flip-flops that all of her friends had, she would torture me until I gave in. But secretly, I wanted to indulge her demands. I wanted her to be happy, to love her mommy who gave her everything. I was slowly creating a live, full-blown entitled beast—a child whose voracious appetite for things, for getting her own way, and for lack of boundaries was out-of-control. I knew that something was terribly wrong but was stuck in the narcissistic pattern of giving in to her "give me, get me, buy me" demands.

Many well-meaning parents bow to the demands of their children early on—not wanting to upset the poor dears. There is a parental fear that not complying with a child's demands will create an angry, frustrated child. Parents fear losing favor with their children. The subliminal message is "If I don't give, I am not a good enough parent." Parents fail to consider the bigger psychological problems that can occur when children lack discipline, boundaries, and humility.

When my child became a teen, the stakes got higher. Forget toys and pink sandals. We're now talking cars and Prada bags. But, with inner strength, a lot of support, and a desire to end the Give Me, Get Me, Buy Me madness, I started to change the entitled child attitude.

In our money-centered society, this has not been an easy task. Parents who I talk with about falling into the entitlement trap utter one overwhelming mantra: "We want to take charge and begin to get control of our families."

Overindulgence is not just about material objects. When we are hesitant to say no to our children for fear that they will withdraw their love or have a tantrum, we are doing ourselves and them a terrible disservice. Children will have a difficult time when they go to school, begin a job, and try to have friendships if they do not have limits and boundaries. Entitled children will always want to come first, and that is not how the real world functions. They will always have a sense of frustration. Parents must take the reigns and monitor their children's activities and not give in so readily to demands. It took me a while to realize the off button is in my hands—not my child's—and in this book, I will help you to press this button.

Give Me, Get Me, Buy Me is a parenting book about the child who says, "I want it now—do everything for me," and the parents who live in a world of mixed messages and confusion. Discipline in today's culture has to be navigated around a blast of media messages and through dozens of technological machines. Children are bombarded with ads, commercials, and hidden product placements. They watch shows about super rich sweet–sixteen birthday parties, spoiled sports stars, and toddlers whose parents spend thousands of dollars on dresses for beauty pageants. Of course, they want it all. It is easy to understand why parents are confused. That is why I wrote this book—to help parents turn these entitled attitudes around.

I know the social, psychological, and discipline messages in *Give Me, Get Me, Buy Me* are the most important ones I will ever share with parents because it is more critical than ever in this competitive world to arm our children with humility, inner strength, resilience, self-assurance, and self-determination so they can be truly happy, productive, and confident.

The following chapters will help parents learn to recognize entitlement traps; make choices that are based on shared respect, understanding, the concept of no, and the recognition of when enough is enough; and to create inner satisfaction in a child who demands "give me, get me, buy me."

CHAPTER ONE

Society and Entitlement

Entitled children act as if they deserve to get what they want, when they want it. All children act that way sometimes, but an entitled child is out of touch with other people's needs and wants because there is an *expectation* that his demands will be met without boundaries. Entitlement is created by good parents who not only overindulge a child, but also send the message that the child is not subject to the same rules as other children, that his needs and wants take precedence over everything else—including themselves. Parents become Give Me, Get Me, Buy Me machines. It is an easy trap to fall into. Not only have I been there, but many of my friends would like to back up and reset the priority buttons, to crack down harder on discipline, and to give more responsibilities in order to teach self-sufficiency.

WHAT IS AN ENTITLED CHILD?

An entitled child possesses certain characteristics which reveal themselves by the time your child is a toddler. We have often observed other parents' entitled children, but rarely do we see these characteristics in our own children. As difficult as this may be, it is both a responsibility and an act of good parenting to be both honest and proactive. The end result will be a balanced, kind, fair, and happy child.

If your child displays at least five of these characteristics, then she is showing entitled behavior:

- Protests and wants his own way: "I won't," "I can't," "I don't want to."
- Doesn't respond to "no" or "stop."
- Doesn't follow rules.
- Doesn't know the difference between her needs and wishes: "I need a new toy," versus "I hope to get a new toy."
- Whines or throws tantrums when he doesn't get his way or you say no.
- Complains constantly.
- Makes unfair or excessive demands: "Get me, give me, buy me."
- Can be bossy or selfish.
- Often doesn't share.

In order to prevent entitled attitudes in children, parents must fully understand their own motivations, actions, and reactions. Not until you are fully cognizant of your past life, and your present parenting style and the motivators behind it, can you have a child who is free from the frustrations and unhappiness produced by entitled attitudes.

The seven traps that lead to entitlement and which we'll discuss are: the "Best" Theory, Rewards for Existence, Attention Getters, the Entitlement Trio, Social Exclusion, Fear of Falling, and Label Lovers. All of these traps are parental and societal pitfalls that are easy to get caught up in. We all want everything for our children. But parents who do not set rules or limits will create children who cannot get satisfied. So, no matter how much you give, it will never be enough.

It is normal for children to ask for things. What creates an entitled child is parents over-responding to their children's wishes, wants, and demands. A parent drops what she's doing to give her child attention, and lets her child believe his needs and wants are more important than other people's. If a parent constantly gives in to a child's demands, buys things in order to placate the child or to give in to societal pressure, and makes faulty decisions in order to not upset the child, then a cycle of entitlement begins.

In this chapter and the succeeding ones, I will help parents stop entitlement traps that lead to negative, spoiled, and demanding behavior. It is important to try and understand where the societal pressures began and how they are perpetuated.

THE "BEST" THEORY

We all want the "best" for our children. But what really is the best? Is the best the best designer clothes? The fanciest crib? The most expensive toys, clothes, or private school? Is it always measured by how much we spend? By someone else's values? Or should best literally be the best we can do?

Is the best always the right choice for your child? What defines the best is obviously subjective, so I asked a hundred parents from various socioeconomic and cultural backgrounds how they defined it. What I found was that in most cases, the parents defined "the best" by how expensive something was or by what other people thought of it. For instance, the best transcends socioeconomic backgrounds: $100 sneakers are demanded by children from wealthy *and* financially depressed backgrounds. These parents didn't want to say no, for fear of their children not fitting in. They didn't want to hear the nagging and arguments, the tears and the guilt. Most of the time saying yes was a lot easier than no.

Meet Lynne. Lynne likes nice things—at least she thought she did until she had a child and joined a Mommy-and-Me group. Her sister-in-law told her to join a particular Mommy-and-Me group because it was the best one in the city. Lynne, knowing virtually nothing about motherhood or Mommy-and-Me, happily took the advice of her sister-in-law who had two children and must be an expert in all things baby.

So, off Lynne went to Mommy-and-Me where she met other mothers. Naturally, the conversations centered on baby issues. "What kind of stroller do you have?" asked one mom. Lynne rattled off the brand of stroller she bought at Target. The mommy was aghast. "I wouldn't use that stroller. I would only buy the best for my baby." Lynne was taken aback. She wanted only the best for her child, too. Had she bought a "less than best" stroller for her darling? She told her husband they had to ditch the Target stroller (which had sold millions), and buy a shiny new one at the local baby boutique for a whopping $600. After all, it was the "best."

The conversation at the next Mommy-and-Me class centered on the topic of toys. One mother suggested that the simple toys from Walmart were not good for her child. Another mom was adamant that the only toys worth having were from the "Toy Boutique for the Sophisticated Baby." Feeling intimidated, Lynne returned her Walmart toys. She headed to the expensive toy boutique and spent $200 on a doll, $100 on a mobile, and $125 on a wooden puzzle (similar to the $20 one she originally bought from Walmart).

At the next class, Lynne learned that a lot of mommies in her class were already applying to elite private nursery schools for their children; some even put in their applications while they were still pregnant. Her baby was barely a year and a half old and not even out of diapers, but poor Lynne was already twelve months behind on the application process. Worse yet, her child would be doomed if she failed to get into one of the best nursery schools. At least, that is what the other mothers told Lynne. Her baby's life would be in shambles. Her child would never reach the status of "best." There would be a social scarlet letter stamped on her child forever.

Ironically enough, the last person to care about the best is the child. In the world of children five and younger, the playing field is even. There is no differentiating among rich, poor, black, red, white, Christian, Jewish, Muslim, Catholic, or "best." Young children are pure social creatures and do not judge people based on their social status, race, or religion—until society bombards them with the notions of social elitism and entitlement. Toddlers are happy to play with pots, pans, dirt, sand, and water. They are thrilled to run around a park or play with a cardboard box and aren't interested in designer labels, private schools, or other status symbols.

In Lynne's case, as in so many other instances, the concept of the best is quickly transferred to the mind of the young child who soaks up the information. Today's parents feel the need to compete and, therefore, give in to the Give Me, Get Me, Buy Me trap, which in turn, teaches their children that they *deserve* things and that the acquisition of things—lots of them—is the best method in one-upping the competition.

Meet Joey, a darling six-year-old who just got a new bike. He has two wonderful, loving parents who have fallen into the "best" trap. They can't stand to see their Joey not having all of the material things that their friends bought for their children. They are worried about being left behind on the social ladder and feel the need to compete for status. The thinking behind this, cites New York psychologist, Donna Moss, is that if I don't give and get enough for my child, then I am a bad parent. I need the outward appearance of love, care, and wealth in order to satisfy inward needs.

Little Joey liked his shiny new bike. But Joey's parents saw that Susie had a bigger one, and Jeffrey had two bikes. Subconsciously Joey's parents projected their feelings of inadequacy onto Joey, causing him to think twice about the bike he was previously so thrilled with. Maybe something was wrong with it. It didn't look so good anymore. Joey lost interest. He now wanted his friend's bicycle—or maybe two bicycles.

His parents, in a frenzy to provide Joey with the best, ran out to get a bigger, shinier bike for Joey. But that new bicycle will only look good until some other model takes its place. When Joey's parents bought Joey a different bike, they sent an unspoken message: "Your choice was not good enough. You need a better one than your friend. Whatever you want, you can have." Joey could not grasp the concept of satisfaction. He was now confused—something better was out there, and he had to have it. His parents, his primary role models, were dissatisfied as well. They indicated that if you don't have bigger, better, best, or more—then you have nothing worth having. Joey just wanted a bike, but commercialism, and social and parental pressures to keep up with others, sent the message "You are not okay until we say so."

Psychologically, humans need to be able to self-soothe and self-satisfy in the face of disappointment or adversity, thereby finding pleasure in individual choices. This has nothing to do with how much money you have, but more with the emphasis and importance you place on money and the messages you give your children. When you can self-satisfy internally as opposed to only getting satisfaction from the external (material things), you build self-confidence and self-efficacy. You are empowered.

REWARDS FOR EXISTENCE

Psychologist Marsha B. Sades, Ph.D., contends that parents can easily train children to be entitled. Aside from the "best theory," society's entitlement model reinforces the idea that our children should be rewarded for simply existing instead of requiring consistent behavior before we dole out privileges. Parents often associate their children reaching a certain age as an occasion for giving, which only digs us deeper into the Give Me, Get Me, Buy Me hole. When our child turns ten, we might buy her a TV; at twelve, a cell phone; and at sixteen, a car. It is okay to get these things. It is the expectation that gets us into trouble. Our "generosity" sends the wrong message to our children that "to exist is to receive."

Giving privileges should not be age-based. Instead, any privilege should be related to competence and responsibility, which will then teach your child that simply existing does not suffice. What matters is *how* he exists—in other words, how he lives his life. By rewarding a child for existing, he has no concept of having to earn or do something to get or maintain a reward.

Some parents give rewards based on their own success. Their child becomes a reflection of their ego, and the more ego-centered the parent, the more entitled the child. The parent wants to show off her accomplishments and may over-indulge and buy things for her child to send a message of financial abundance. The child feels he has a "right" to rewards, which completely negates the meaning of reward in the first place. The dictionary defines the word *reward* as "something given or received in return or as recompense for service, merit, hardship, etc." In the case of rewards for existence, this definition goes out the window completely.

According to Dr. Sades, parents who indulge children by rewarding them for simply existing believe:

1) My child deserves to be happy all the time.

2) My child should be protected from any problems or deprivation.

By utilizing this parenting model, the entitled child begins to take on her own beliefs:

1) My life should be fun.

2) You owe me what I need to have an easy, happy life.

3) I am angry when privileges are taken away from me.

Clearly, no parent sets out to raise an entitled child. We often think that we are doing the best for our children. But in the quest to give, we often become indulgent and can inadvertently create an angry, belligerent, lazy child—one who has his parents hopping around making sure his every wish is granted. Children don't necessarily want to be this way, but if they don't learn alternative behaviors, then entitled children is what they'll become. Other children and adults will often not tolerate such entitled behaviors. The "real world" may not be so indulgent.

ATTENTION GETTERS

Wailing, crying, shuddering, silent treatments—these are some of the attention-getting behaviors that children exhibit when they don't get what they want. These tactics can easily wear down parents and cause them to give in to their children. Some parents simply cannot tolerate listening to their children cry and whine at the thought of hurting their feelings, so they give, get, and buy for the sake of their nerves and quiet in the home. Entitled attitudes are anchored in this parenting behavior. By responding to the child's attention-getting behaviors, you instill a self-centered attitude in the child. She thinks that the positive reinforcement you give her for negative behavior is due to the fact that she has called attention to herself, even if she needed to use a negative way to get the attention.

Some children, who are so used to getting their needs met immediately without delayed gratification, become irate if they are told no or to wait. This child yells, "You are not fair," and he truly believes if he does not get what he wants that he was gypped. According to psychologist Nancy Lynne Namka, Ed.D., on an unconscious level this child not only believes what happened to him was not fair, but he believes that he is owed. Dr. Namka cites that when early dependency needs are not provided sufficiently, the child feels a sense of loss that manifests itself in anger. The child may react continuously to perceived small injustices in daily life by having no strong inner self to defend against problems that arise. A child who feels owed and who is always making demands will push people away. His defenses are up, and he will get mad and have a tantrum in order to manipulate and get what he wants.

This child cannot self-soothe. That is why it is so important to teach children from infancy self-soothing by:

• Allowing a child to cry for a short while in order to
  get to sleep.

- Giving transitional objects (things like blankets or stuffed animals that provide comfort) to infants.

- Not placating a tantrum by giving in to your child's demands.

Let her learn to calm herself down or be prepared to follow through with appropriate consequences such as a time-out and/or leaving a store, playdate, park. These methods will teach a child that life is a series of ups and downs, and how one copes with the disappointments is the key to getting through life.

By constantly rescuing your child by giving in, you can build his frustration. Children who are always entertained or mollified do not learn to delay gratification and continually make demands. Don't misunderstand: attention is good for children. But the attention can be harmful if it is excessive, given at the wrong time, or given immediately at the expense of your own needs. A child should learn to do things for himself, and too much attention can get in the way of self-reliance.

When you are working or in the middle of doing a task and you drop everything to give your child attention (as long as he is not hurt), you are giving the wrong message. If your child is whining or throwing a tantrum and you immediately try to placate your child, you are giving incorrect attention, and your child won't learn to wait. She will expect you to jump when she calls. Both parent and child can exclude others by becoming self-focused. This is not good for a child who needs to learn social skills to get along with other children, to respect adults, and to listen to parents.

Be aware: paying attention to infants is critical. Holding babies and giving attention is not spoiling. Parents in many cultures hold babies all day. In fact, experts say you cannot spoil an infant, especially prior to six months of age. This is because it isn't until about the six-month mark that infants start recognizing cause and effect. It is when a child passes this point and has cognitive understanding of yes and no that parents run the risk of overindulgence. Children beyond the age of about six months starts to realize that when they cry, they get picked up. Associations are made at this age, and they take that understanding of cause and effect into toddlerhood and start experimenting with negative behaviors, like tantrums. The key to avoiding this is to give appropriate levels of attention, and not set everything aside every time your child asks, give me, get me, buy me.

THE ENTITLEMENT TRIO

Fostering entitlement encompasses three specific parenting behaviors:

• Overindulgence

• Lack of boundaries

• Overprotecting

The entitlement trio comes from loving and good intentions but can have negative consequences on a child. David J. Bredehoft, Ph.D., a professor of psychology and coauthor of *How Much Is Enough?*, was the director of the Overindulgence Project (Dawson, Bredehoft & Clarke, 2004; Bredehoft, 2007). Three hundred sixty-nine adults from thirty-seven states and nine countries were polled. He completed two questionnaires: The Aspiration Index, which measured External Aspirations—wealth, fame, and image—and Internal Aspirations, which measured meaningful relationships, personal growth, and charitable acts. The second questionnaire measured parental overindulgence from the view of the child. In his study, Dr. Bredehofdt concluded that "too much overindulgence (clothes, toys, and privileges) was the major culprit to having children grow up greedy, self-centered, and never satisfied." He found that overindulgence can negatively affect learning, motivation, and personal relationships.

This fascinating study revealed that overindulgence consisted of three acts: giving too much (material objects, privileges, activities, toys), overprotecting (not allowing your child to learn by trial and error but rather doing everything for him), and lack of structure (being too easy, not setting boundaries, no consistent enforcement of rules).

The study found children with intrinsic goals had better self-esteem, more motivation, and were generally happier with their lives. They had purpose. Dr. Bredehoft noted that when parents overindulge, their children tend to put the emphasis on extrinsic goals. The child becomes self-centered and unable to see the world outside of his needs. This entitlement trio will be addressed throughout the book. The three acts form the basis of entitlement attitudes.

SOCIAL EXCLUSION

As your child grows, so does her world of school, friendships, community, and activities. Her experience in this world can be rich with sharing, bullying behavior, unhappy social relationships, learning new things from others, and fun times with friends. It can also be fraught with bossiness and frustration if your child does not learn to give and take, wait, listen, share, and compromise. An entitled child often isolates people by acting as if her needs should be met over other people's. We have all witnessed the child who pushes in front of others, interrupts, refuses to follow the teacher's directions, argues with coaches, and is insensitive to others' feelings. These traits, if left unchecked, will socially exclude your child.

Entitled children can push other children away with an attitude of superiority and bossiness. The entitled child doesn't like to share because he wants all the goodies for himself. Entitled kids want to hoard attention, material goods, and top spots.

Before full maturity, children see the world from a narcissistic perspective. Their world is all about them. Usually, we outgrow this self-involvement by our late teens. But you can help your child develop a social conscience. As children can pay a social price for entitled behavior, it is vital to teach them to get along with others so they can have satisfying relationships.

An honest assessment of your child's strengths and weaknesses actually provides her with a better chance at success. By acknowledging the good with the bad, you can truly appreciate who your child really is and nurture all that is good—in both character and talents. Help your child build self-confidence and a solid belief system.

Take some time to evaluate your child's personal traits using the categories that follow. Rate your child's ability or level on a scale of one (at the low end) to ten (at the high end). Allow your child to do a self-assessment as well. Do not direct him. It is important to see how your child views himself. You may not be aware that he sees himself as academically or sports challenged, for instance. Use this as an open forum for an honest family discussion.

Personal Traits	Parent Assessment	Child Self-Assessment (School Age)
	Give a rating between 1–10. 1 is the low end and 10 is the high end.	
Overall Academics		
Sports		
Social Skills, Manners, Friendliness		
Musical Ability		
Artistic Talent		
Mechanical Skills		
Verbal Skills		
Empathy (to feel what others feel)		
Kindness and Caring		
Charity		
Emphasis on Extrinsic Goals		
Emphasis on Intrinsic Goals		

The chart is a way to reevaluate balance and appreciation. By emphasizing the positive character traits in your child and not pushing him or chastising him for not getting perfect grades or being the best athlete, your child will have a chance to reach his personal best rather than unrealistic goals and will see himself more realistically. Entitled children are often out-of-touch with tangible facts because they believe they are better and entitled. It is okay for your child to be "average." This does not make him less, especially if he excels in personal traits like empathy and caring. These are the traits that should be emphasized.

FEAR OF FALLING

Some parents show overprotective behavior from the first time their child skins her knee by falling off her bike. The parent whisks her off to the doctor or forbids her from riding her bike ever again. Parents who react this way may be doing more harm than good.

David Brooks, *New York Times* op-ed columnist and author, chronicles overachieving "boomlets" (children of baby boomers) in his book *Bobos in Paradise*. He found that these children, for the most part, are bright, hard-working, and social. So, why worry? Doesn't every parent want a child who possesses these characteristics?

The problem, Brooks explains, is that "We may be robbing

our children of the experience of being children because of both our inability to let our children fall, bang and scrape themselves, and because parents avert any chance of child failure to avoiding risk at all costs." A parent's overprotection reinforces the child's feeling of entitlement by eliminating the possibility of failure from the child's life. The child can't fail, because he's not put in a position in which to fail.

Parents can also overprotect their children because of their preoccupation with their children's futures. "A broken arm, once a badge of courageous rambunctious play, is now seen as a child whose college baseball career might be endangered because of a slow-to-heal arm," Brooks notes.

Overprotecting robs a child of independence and self-efficacy. Use these parenting tools to avoid overprotecting:

- Let your child try new tasks as long as they are safe and healthy.
- Give your child responsibility at home and don't criticize her.
- Don't get hysterical every time your child falls or fails at something.
- Don't force your child to do an activity he dislikes. Not every child is going to be a star athlete or rocket scientist.

By being overprotective, parents can unwittingly create an overly anxious and fearful child. In the book, *The Blessing of the Skinned Knee,* Wendy Mogel, Ph.D., explains that a child feels as if the world is not a safe place if you panic every time she falls, gets a fever, or doesn't do well at something. The subliminal message here is "Something terrible is happening." A child can become overly anxious and fearful. It is important to find your child's positive traits and nurture them as well as having a realistic picture of when to react.

GOING OVERBOARD

Many parents feel they need to go overboard with their children's parties and gifts to impress friends and help make their children socially accepted and popular. For example, when Casey turned seven, her parents gave her an elaborate birthday party complete with pony rides, a clown, a magician, and goody bags that were more expensive than most of Casey's gifts. Casey had few friends, but her parents invited fifty children and threw an expensive party hoping it would help Casey socially.

Turned off by Casey's bragging, the other children called Casey a spoiled brat behind her back but accepted invitations to fancy play dates. Furthermore, Casey's parents' actions sent her the message that you could gain friends by impressing them with expensive things.

Casey's parents are not unique. We live in a society where what we have is perceived as more important than who we are.

People are too concerned with where they live, the size of their houses, and the cars they drive. Parents reinforce this kind of thinking in their children by modeling behavior that teaches their children to judge people's worth by the size of their parties or the gifts they can afford to give.

Some parents go so far as to choose their children's friends based on their parents' favorable financial status. They only want their child to associate with children in families of certain financial means. It doesn't matter if the child's playmates are smart, funny, or nice, as long as they're monetarily privileged.

Living by these standards, we diminish our own self-worth. When we spend so much time and energy competing to impress others, we surely set ourselves up for failure because our energy goes into extrinsic goals rather than accomplishing our best. The social bar can always be raised higher and higher by someone richer, better looking, and more prominent. Then what happens? Are we less when we can't compete on as high a level as we did previously? Of course not.

Still, our society instills in us the desire to acquire things. Many people forsake relationships, time with their family, and sometimes their own health for the sake of the mighty dollar. They justify their actions by saying they work so hard to provide the best for their families. In truth, their children lose out on the most important things, things that money cannot buy— time with their parents and solid values on which to grow. Rather than spending time with their children and paying attention to them, parents often buy them things, which inevitably creates a void in the child's life. The child then strives to get more things to fill up the void.

A child needs to know what ideals are important to make choices that will shape his life and view of the world. The pull of a society consumed with the obsession of money and social position sometimes is difficult to overcome.

LABEL LOVERS

We have become a culture of designer labels: Gucci, Prada, Armani, Chanel. The media sells style and labels as a mark of honor, and yes, I am a creature of these same label lovers. Children beg for expensive tennis shoes, purses, backpacks, jackets—all with labels. Labels define our life because they signify a type of social acceptance—the ultimate mark of entitlement. As a culture, we thrive on others' approval. By seeking others' approval, you can lose sight of what you want and define yourself by what others think you should have. If others define who you are, you can lose your sense of self.

This is especially true of young people whose sense of self isn't fully formed—they're incredibly impressionable. If a child follows the group, striving for approval, without being true to her beliefs, she becomes more interested in what others think of her, rather than discovering what she, herself, thinks.

Labels act as an unspoken definition of who we are, how much we have, what we value. By giving a child labels at an early age, you are not giving him the ability to define himself. A young tween can feel inferior if she does not have the right purse or shoes that all the other girls own. This is normal because tweens want to fit in and be a part of the group. But there is a limit to label demons.

It is when parents start to indulge label fantasies and puts emphasis on price tags that the child is set apart. At thirteen, my daughter's friend would come to school with a Gucci bag and Chanel shoes. Not until this girl let the other girls know the cost of these labels did any of them care. Once they knew, she had status, which put pressure on the other tweens.

Label lovers can be avoided by simple tools:

- Explain what is important.
- Help your child to define his own sense of style and taste.
- Give your younger child two choices when shopping.
- Ask your older child to make a list of what her desires are. Let her know your budget before your shop, and don't go over the amount.
- Let your child know shopping does not always mean buying.
- Teach the value of finding sale or less expensive items. If you find a bargain, put some of the money saved (for

example, $5) in your child's piggy bank and stress the importance of saving, finding great buys, and looking good for less.

Parents who obsess about possessions and strive to own the right designer clothes, cars, computers, and cell phones inadvertently teach their children to admire and desire the same material things. Some women will spend hundreds or even thousands of dollars on a purse with a certain label that immediately sends the message that it is expensive. A daughter who watches her mother take pleasure in such a purchase will learn to want designer goods to make a statement about herself.

As adults, we believe that attaining the "right" material things and being part of the "right" group will boost our self-esteem. We equate symbols with success. In truth, building self-esteem is an internal, not external job. Validation that "I'm okay" must come from one's self by constantly giving value to people—not things—as well as education, family, and giving. These values should be discussed daily and modeled in your home. Children begin to develop self-esteem when they see within their parents positive reinforcement, acceptance, and unconditional love. As we grow, we internalize that acceptance and develop self-love.

It is important for your child to grow up with an internalized value system that he can fall back on as he grows. Therefore, it is up to you, as a parent, to create a strong sense of what is important. The value of people should take precedence over things. A sense of responsibility to the community and to family is more important than a new toy. Children need to know that designer labels go in and out of fashion, but human values will serve them well for their entire lives.

Children gain strength from parents who are strong, structured, and strict. You have to decide if it is easier "to give, to get, and to buy," and pay the consequences, or if you're up for challenging your child's entitled attitudes. If your choice is the latter, read on.

CHAPTER TWO

Parental Entitlement Traps

We all have parental pitfalls at sometime or another. We can fail to recognize our behavior and how it affects our children. In Chapter 1, you learned about societal traps. But the more profound traps are the emotional ties, both between your parents and your child. These emotional ties are the basis for our character and healthy relationships.

BUTTON PUSHERS

There is a line from an old television show where a woman says, "How come my parents can push all my buttons?" The husband answers, "That's easy. They installed them." This aha moment hits a deep nerve in all of us. Parents are the primary psychological model in our lives until we reach adolescence. But it truly never ends; we are influenced by parental power our entire lives. Their input is filled with wants, shoulds, cannots, wishes, approvals, hurts, joys, fears, and love. The buttons are charged with positives and negatives and can misfire at any time with a parental comment or deed. Parents and children can bring about emotions in each other that you didn't think possible.

Some buttons push too far, and the triggers evoke unresolved anger. Emotional buttons from our past can lead us to overindulge our own children by pulling us into the place of deprived reaction. This leads to an attitude of "I will give more than I got. I will be indulgent because I felt deprived. I didn't have, so I will give everything. I will show you!"

ATTACHMENT

It is natural through modeling to take on the characteristics and traits of our parents. Parenting styles are passed down from one generation to the next, and negative behaviors often become ingrained in our children and our children's children. New studies suggest that early, stable, and warm connections with children will create positive qualities in the child as she matures. Stability is based on predictable and consistent behavior by a parent. This encompasses active and passive play, eye contact, physical bonding, and meeting early infant needs. Those parents who are anxious and overly indulgent will foster children who will become anxious and overindulgent.

HEALTHY SEPARATION

According to D. W. Winnicott, a prominent developmental child psychologist, in early infancy a child needs constant nurturing and gratification to create a healthy bond with his parent. When a child reaches toddlerhood, the parent should start a process called disillusionment in her child. The parent needs to send the message by her actions that her child cannot have everything he wants. By setting limits and not letting a child cling, whine, cry, and throw a tantrum when he is not getting his way, he will learn that mom cannot do what he wants all the time, and that he can self-soothe. Conversely, if limits are not set, the child will grow to become greedy and spoiled by constantly demanding attention.

The stages for distinct separation occur twice in a child's life, during toddlerhood and during adolescence. Even with a healthy separation, children experience fears, anger, disassociation, withdrawal, and tantrums while going through the process. During toddler separation, a child learns that her parents are separate entities. She begins to move away from the umbilical love object (mother) and finds interest in children, toys, perhaps a sibling, and other family members. Physical, emotional, and psychological changes occur during adolescent separation as the preteen develops friendships outside of the family unit, including those of a romantic nature.

Part of attachment is being able to detach, or separate, in a healthy way. People with attachment issues have typically struggled with attachment in their childhood. Deprivation of attention and early bonding can lead to the child who cannot get satisfied. This drives the individual to focus on external gratifications (acquisitions), and external objects become substitutes for love. Instead of being bonded, the relationship has "material objects" in the middle. Parent and child react to the object as opposed to each other.

Physician and psychoanalyst Margaret Mahler's theory of attachment has inspired an entire field of psychology that studies a child's bond to his primary parent(s) or caregiver. For Mahler, that is the mother. She stresses the importance of early, consistent attentiveness during the child's first three years of life as being vital to the ultimate goals of raising an adaptable adult. With healthy attachment, the parent is able to free herself from guilt, hovering, overindulgence, and over-identification because she feels secure in her relationship to her child. Both parent and child can function independently and then join together without anxiety or fear.

The following is a set of healthy adult-child parameters that will help parents avoid the traps of entitlement and attach in a healthy way:

- **Be proactive.** It is important to anticipate your child's needs and expectations and to let him know the limitations and rules ahead of time. Set down rules with each stage of your child's growth. This puts the parent power in your hands and heads off conflict. Don't wait to set up rules when he is in the middle of a tantrum.

- **Everybody wins.** Offer your child choices (usually two), and encourage cooperation. This avoids permissiveness by everyone feeling satisfied.

- **Set for success.** By giving clear directions that are oriented to your child's age level and her learning style, you help her to be successful without pushing or setting her up for failure by having unrealistic expectations. For example, if your child does not meet your academic expectations, don't act like she is "not smart" but rather encourage her positive traits and offer solutions, like a tutor.

- **Catch them being good.** Focus on what your child is doing right and build on his strengths. Give rewards for positive behavior, good listening, following directions, helping, sharing. Give him incentives and positive reinforcement. If you tell him that you appreciate his help and good behavior, he'll take notice.

- **Do as I say.** Do not expect from your child what you don't expect from yourself. Maintain consistent behavior so your child can have predictable expectations of parental behavior, thereby following the modeling. For example, if you tell your child not to leave her clothes on the floor and you leave your clothes on the floor, you are giving mixed messages.

• **Show affection.** Do not punish punitively or withdraw affection when your child does not obey. Avoid useless warnings and delayed consequences or praise. The more you emotionally withdraw, the more your child will whine and make demands to get your attention.

• **Don't be a fixer.** The entitled child wants you to "fix" everything and solve problems. Support your child's feelings, but do not dismiss them, fix them, or constantly give advice. This can create entitled attitudes. Allow your child to learn by his mistakes. You create entitlement by never letting your child fail and always making sure nothing is out of place.

By practicing these principles, you can set the process of parent-child attachment in motion. Parents can promote emotional security in their children by fostering emotional and physical communication. On the other hand, an insecure parent may give in and placate her child's demands. This "giving in" can create an angry parent and a child who will manipulate and whine to get attention.

By using the techniques above, you will encourage the development of an involved, as opposed to self-involved, child;

one who listens rather than demands; who is a participant rather than the center of attention; who takes pleasure in helping and giving—not just getting.

There is another area where parents can get trapped into separating the child and parent experience. This is called overidentification.

OVERIDENTIFICATION

Overidentification is a term for confusion over our parental roles and overinvolvement in our children's lives. When you overidentify, you and your child both become enmeshed in your child's experiences, and you fail to separate your child from yourself.

Unintentionally, parents can become overly involved with their children. One mom I know found herself over-involved in her fourteen-year-old daughter's social life. By using her daughter's e-mail address, the mother secretly posed as her daughter and sent nasty messages to children who she felt were not nice to her child. She would engage in online gossip about her daughter's classmates. Instead of allowing her daughter to have her own social exchange and to learn how to navigate relationships, the mother interfered on a very personal level. The mother took on the social experience as if it were her own. She felt entitled to intrude into her daughter's life.

I have observed kids on sports fields with parents who harass coaches, yell at other children, and interfere in their children's playing because they feel that the sports experience is theirs as much as their children's. For example, a dad named Barry couldn't stand to see his son, Gerry, do poorly in baseball. Each time Gerry struck out or missed the ball, Barry would throw his hands up in exasperation. He yelled at Gerry, "What's wrong? We aren't hitting very well today." He berated the coach for poor instruction. He yelled at the pitcher for trying to hit Gerry. He screamed at other players. Barry sent the message, "You don't have to do well because you are entitled. Everyone else is playing poorly." So Gerry took on this attitude that everyone else was wrong but him. Barry not only shifted responsibility, but got overly involved in his child's activity.

For children to grow, they must learn from their own mistakes and successes. Some children can become overly dependent on their parents and frightened to make decisions for fear of parental disapproval.

When a parent has trouble "letting go," he may coddle his child from harm and shelter her from free interaction with other children, thereby impeding the natural growth process. Children learn by making mistakes and trying new things. When a parent constantly intervenes, a child may second-guess her choices and become fearful of making a wrong decision or disappointing her parent, thereby causing her to constantly look to her parent to make decisions and rescue her when she cannot cope.

When you overidentify with your children, you send them the message that they are more important than anyone else. The child then develops a narcissistic attitude and loses empathy for others—only relating to the world from his own perspective.

SELF-INVOLVEMENT

Many people feel they are owed a good life—an indulged life. There is a constant sense that life is not fair. There is the internal voice that says, "If I don't get my own way and if I don't get what I want, I will get angry." This type of behavior can continue well into adulthood where demands and an entitled attitude can cause a person to lose friendships and jobs. In her article, "You Owe Me! Children of Entitlement," parenting author Dr. Nancy Lynne Namka, Ed.D., points out that as a needy, overindulged child becomes an adult, he learns to "substitute anger, meanness, addictive substances, workaholic behavior, or material objects to fill his neediness."

Children want to get along, ask for what they want in a reasonable manner, and bond with parents in a positive way. You can help your child make changes. You can reverse the effects of selfish and entitled behavior by reflecting on your own life and parental influences.

There are mistakes in parenting that can be reversed no matter how old or young your child. Some of the most prevalent entitled attitudes focus on self-involved children and parents. These attitudes carry over to your children, but you can alter them by becoming aware of the behaviors and changing parental interaction.

Self-Involved Attitudes

The following list highlights self-involved attitudes that can carry over from parent to child:

- **Delayed gratification.** This child is like the character Veruca Salt in *Charlie and the Chocolate Factory* who declares, "Daddy, I want it now!" This child can become upset easily when her needs are not being met. The unconscious thinking is "I'm special. Give me what I want, or you don't really love me, and I will withhold my love."

- **Lack of empathy.** This child is so enmeshed in his own neediness that his thinking revolves only around him, and he does not have the ability to put himself in another person's place. He exists to be gratified and can be insensitive to other people's feelings.

- **Anger and triggers.** This child has angry outbursts when she doesn't get what she wants. She uses anger and tantrums to manipulate her parents and keep them "off" track. The cycle continues as the child promises to be good, but then gets angry when she doesn't get what she wants.

- **Blame.** This child blames everyone else for his unhappiness. He is unwilling to take personal responsibility, and everyone else is making him miserable.

- **Center of self.** This child wants to be the center of attention, and when she is not, she feels devalued. She believes herself to be more special than others and feels she deserves the biggest and the best, always without sharing.

Self-involved children have trouble seeing anything beyond getting their own way. The parental job is to teach empathy and social skills and to help the child become a part of the whole family structure, not the nucleus. You want to teach thinking and feeling skills. To do so, you must first recognize where you might inadvertently feed into your child's entitled behavior. You might be unknowingly contributing to his defensive, needy actions.

WAYS TO STOP SELF-INVOLVED ATTITUDES

Consider trying the following strategies to stop self-involved attitudes in your child:

- **Specialness.** Do not constantly say to your child, "You are special." This child will feel she doesn't always have to follow the rules and she is better than other kids. It is fine to find special qualities in your child, but by comparing her to others and making her feel superior, she may get a false sense of entitlement. Be realistic, and help her to find good qualities in others.

- **Distraction.** Don't give in to your child and constantly protect him from his own feelings. Sometimes a child has to experience different feelings—anger, disappointment, happiness. He can't always have every need met by a parent who is trying to shelter him.

- **Snap.** Don't engage in daily power struggles that lead to anger. Don't let your child beat you down until you snap and say yes. This child will push you until you are beaten down. Nip this behavior early, give a warning, and if the pushing does not stop, implement a punishment (for example, time out, take away privileges).

- **Overanalyzing.** Don't constantly reason and talk to your child about why she can't have something. Sometimes, a no is a no. Do not engage. Walk away.

- **Projection.** Don't show your own anxiety and vulnerability when you stand your ground and refuse your child's requests. Don't ask, "Is this okay? Do you mind?" Be consistent. Use a strong voice and say, "Because I am the parent." Remember you know more, have lived longer, and are smarter and stronger.

The hope for the entitled child is to provide him with training to help him view his world differently by:

- Learning to follow directions and take in information instead of going to instant debate.

- Delaying gratification and learning to inhibit impulsive actions.

- Learning to separate the big deals from the little deals and let go of the small injustices of life.

- Learning to create boundaries and allow others their boundaries.

- Dealing with frustrations in socially acceptable ways.

- Reinforcing her own self when behavior is appropriate.

- Becoming his own advocate for making good choices.

- Viewing others with empathy and seeing things from their point of view.

It is important for the parent and child to develop a healthy type of relationship based on the balance between giving and receiving. According to Los Angeles psychologist, Jill Model Barth, Ph.D., when interviewed, revealed, "The wish to belong and fit in are usually parents' projections of their own fear of rejection and abandonment that comes from their own childhood." As Dr. Model Barth explains, "This calls into question the function children provide for some parents, narcissistic expressions of themselves. If a child does not live up to the narcissistic expression, then the parent criticizes. The parent feels 'less' because he perceives himself as less. Criticism is a type of control. A parent who pushes through criticism is fearful of losing love from his child. He controls to maintain dependence. But eventually the child will rebel out of anger, and the parent will be emotionally abandoned again replaying his childhood trauma. This all leads to the parent and child feeling hurt and ultimately owed more love and attention." By putting yourself in the position of parent/caretaker, you can see yourself in a mature, responsible role as opposed to being a parent/child to your child.

EARLY PAIN

These powerful reactors can only hurt, not help your child. Most of us begin the parenting process with positive and loving intentions, but the pain of early childhood trauma, disapproval, anger, or criticism can intrude into the parenting process. The early development of a child is a complex interactive process.

The child is shaped by her environment (nature) and the parents' interaction with her (nurture). The way you respond to your child in part is determined by how you were responded to. It is vital to come to terms with early behavior, so you will not repeat this negative emotional behavior with your children.

Early behavioral patterns set the groundwork for how we parent. If issues are left unresolved, they can have unforeseen negative effects on your child. We tend to parent much like our parents and their parents before them. We either embrace or reject these negative effects. If there are unhealthy interactions and poor bonding, this can carry over from one generation to the next.

When Nathan was a child, he was willing to do anything to please his father but could not succeed. Nathan learned quickly that if he displayed any anger or negative feelings around his father, he was punished. So Nathan started having temper tantrums. He was willing to get negative attention simply to connect with his father. His only outlets for his stifled feelings were at school and on the playing field. At one point he was expelled for hitting a boy with a baseball. His father pulled further away from Nathan. This early imprint was very powerful. Nathan repeated this pattern when he became an adult and punished his own son, Josh, for expressing angry feelings. Josh could not express his anger openly, so he would hit and scream when he did not get his own way. He became a bully.

Amy is another example of early pain. Amy could never please her mother. Each accomplishment was always met with the attitude that she could do better. If she got Bs or Cs on her report card, her mother would go to school and complain about the lousy teachers, the terrible books, the incompetent school system. She made excuses for Amy and blamed others. This pattern continued into Amy's own life. She would never take responsibility for her actions and subsequently she blamed others for her grades and her disappointments. Amy followed the negative parental pattern.

Not until we deal with unresolved issues can we break the conditioned bonds of generational-patterned behavior. These patterns are what cause us to overindulge our children—we do so to make up for feelings of hurt, and we suppress openness and acceptance. And the cycle only stops with your awareness of the past and of how you were influenced by parental approval or disapproval. This understanding of your own life helps because it can clarify areas that cause you to act in ways that create an entitled child.

In order to recognize if you have negative patterns, ask yourself:

- Do I get angry often at my child and my spouse?
- Do I feel guilty when I am away from my child often?
- Did I have a critical, controlling parent?
- Am I critical?

• Do I have inflated expectations of myself and my child?

• Do I think my child or I am better than most people?

If you find yourself answering yes to or identifying with these questions, read on to find productive ways to break the negative patterns.

BREAKING THE PATTERNS

It is important to break from the negative patterns of conditional behavior from your own childhood. Remember:

• **Don't be too hard on yourself.** You are trying to become a better parent. You cannot hold onto self-anger if you want to move on positively. Forgive your own parents so you can move forward.

• **Define what you want to change.** For instance, *I want to stop being critical of my child every time he gets a grade lower than an A.* If you start to become critical, stop and backup. Say you are sorry, and rephrase your intentions.

• **Let things go.** Do not focus on every negative aspect of your behavior or your child's. Be willing to give up certain issues. Pick your battles. No one is perfect—not even you.

- **Don't be defensive.** Your child may annoy you to get your attention. You are the adult. Find out what she really wants.

- **Be aware of your actions.** Chart how many times a day you display positive and negative behavior toward your child. Awareness of negative patterns will allow you to break these same patterns by seeing what areas you want to change and how often you repeat the behaviors.

UNCONSCIOUS SELF

Not only is it important to be aware of parental patterns, but it is also important to be aware of negative messages we send to our children through our "unconscious self." These messages form part of our child's ego. The unconscious self also reflects the world around us and thus functions in the world in a particular way—aggressive, possessive, overly competitive, manipulative, honest, trustworthy. If a parent is not clear as to what human traits are important, then his child may be equally confused.

There is faulty thinking in the concept that if you excel in a particular area, you are either a superior human or a better person. Some parents *unconsciously* instill in their child the idea that if you are good at something (sports, arts, academics), then you are good. The child may come to believe that her talents or genetics are what make her a good person. However, it's important to stress the human tools for success. This is a difficult concept to grasp, especially in light of today's faulty heroes whom society has held up to undeserved adoration.

For instance, athletes, who were once revered for their kindness, good deeds, compassion, and role model images, now make headlines for spousal abuse, drug charges, use of steroids, and beating up coaches and referees. They feel entitled to misbehave because their athletic talent is continually rewarded with money and adulation. These competitive gladiators are the people your children look up to. In films and video games, the tough guy is the hero. Reality stars feel entitled to act spoiled because their lives are held up like mirrors that often reflect the worst in our behavior. But we accept this behavior—and even condone it by big ratings. These are some of the role models who have been accepted by our society and by your children.

Do not accept faulty role models. Be honest about heroes' good and bad qualities. Try to point out characteristics that make a true hero: honesty, kindness, generosity.

It is okay to moralize—there is not enough in our society. There is a line between bad and good behavior.

SELF-CONFRONTATION

Ultimately, you cannot be productive or giving toward your child if you do not care about and give to yourself.

Many parents who have grown up with feelings of not being valued and not feeling good about who they are transfer these feelings onto their children. This continues unless the negative cycle is broken. It is imperative to begin to give yourself both love and understanding. This begins with a willingness to forgive your parents for what you perceive as a lack of care on their part.

It is important to understand that care is not defined here as meeting one's basic needs of clothes, shelter, and food. Lack of care is defined as an emotional absence—when a parent does not meet the psychological needs of a child by withdrawing love and attention. This may have happened without full knowledge of the emotional ramifications, but the scars go deep. A critical parent, a controlling parent, or a withdrawn parent can negatively affect how you live your whole life.

If every time you look for approval you are criticized, you will grow up self-critical because that is how you were conditioned. You will feel devalued. Many people overcompensate by using bravado. They act overconfident, cocky, even narcissistic in order to veil their real feelings of incompetence and insecurity. This translates into an attitude of entitlement.

In Dina's case, her mother was emotionally cold and withdrawn. She emphasized Dina's looks and clothing choices. Dina was constantly trying to get her mother's attention and love. She did everything to please her mom. She was the good girl, excelling in school, athletics, and socializing. But this did not change her mother's attitude.

When Dina had children, she constantly indulged her two sons with material objects. She met their every desire. Her overriding goal was to be the nurturing mother she longed for. By not repairing herself emotionally, Dina overcompensated. To give materially is a symbol for the wish to receive gratification of internal needs.

As Los Angeles psychoanalyst Dr. Model Barth says, "We often long to make up for what we didn't get from our own mothers. Therefore, Dina tended to overgive to her children." When Dina gave to her children, unconsciously she was the child who was being given love and attention. Dina was trying to make reparations for her mother's emotional distance by substituting her children for herself. She was still longing for a warm, nurturing mother. Dina would be able to make peace with her mother and herself only when she extricated herself from her mother's emotional hold.

Dr. Model Barth explains that Dina's mother's coldness gave her a sense of control and power. Her mother existed on negative energy, observing how hard people worked to get her attention and approval. This gave her a sense of control over her life, which was internally chaotic. So, in actuality, Dina's mother was incapable of connecting. Her mother could not sustain a connection to meet Dina's needs.

For Dina to repair the relationship with herself and thereby help her children become psychologically healthy, she needs an awareness that the overgratifying behavior is a reaction to the deprivation she felt as a child. Dina needs clarification. She can get this either through therapy or self-realization, so she can deal with her feelings of loss.

Dina also needs self-confrontation. She needs to confront the deeper meaning of her behavior and what she hopes the behavior will gratify. She also can directly confront her mother, but this is a more difficult task since her mother is the source of her emotional pain and may not be receptive to listening.

Finally, Dina needs to work through the feelings of loss associated with longings and wishes for her internal needs to be gratified. She has to deal with her own emotions so she doesn't transfer them onto her children.

No matter how much she tries, Dina will always relate to her mother by virtue of identification with the same-sex parent. That is, her mother, being female, has an enormous influence on Dina's role as a woman, wife, and mother. Dina has imprinted much of her mother's behavioral patterns because she gender-identifies with her just like a boy would pattern his father's behavior.

It is normal to model the same-sex parent. The problems occur when the parent displays negative behaviors that the child overidentifies with and then carries these behaviors into adulthood and into his role as a parent. It is important to recognize negative behaviors that parents exhibit in order to individuate and gain awareness of behaviors that can hurt both yourself and your child. Examples of negative behaviors include:

- **Overcompensation.** Overgiving in order to make up for unresolved feelings of not having received enough love, attention, and positive reinforcement.

- **Retaliation.** Psychologically "getting back" at your parent or child for emotional damage done to you. This is a primitive form of defense motivated by rage. It's a rigid style of dealing with hurt and anger, and the only way a person feels she can get back at her parent is through revenge. But it is manifested through her own child. Most of the time the feelings are unconscious.

- **Intertwined.** Some people never really separate from their parents and see them as their primary emotional source. Thus, they never develop an independent relationship with their own children because they are still dependent on their parents for guidance.

Dina will need to recognize her negative patterns and rebuild with positive patterns. By doing so, she will be giving her children the real gift—herself.

Self-giving is not achieved quickly or without some price. When giving to yourself, other aspects of yourself may have to be given up. Internal self-giving replaces material and overin-flated entitled self-giving. Even negative behavior becomes comfortable, if that is all you are used to. Self-giving requires change, but a positive change, one that will improve your life forever. Once you have gained awareness of negative behavior patterns, you can engage in building positive behaviors that can lead to healthier relationships and ultimately better parenting.

By rebuilding positive behaviors with your own parents, you set the framework for your own healing. Some of the best ways to do this are:

- **Engage in confrontation.** Positive rebuilding is possible through open communication. Confront your own behavior and search for the meaning behind your negative feelings. Tell your parents what hurt you and allow them to explain, apologize, or say nothing.

- **Let go of expectations.** Let go of the hopes for a fantasy life and relationship that will never be. Let go of patterns that negatively affect you and your own child. Work on yourself, and that will reflect on those you love.

- **Rebuild.** Make amends psychologically in order to break free of the negative cycle of parent identification. Take the opportunity with people in your present life to work through your feelings. For example, when you are in a struggle with your child, you tend to replicate what is in your past. Stay aware, and if necessary, apologize to your child for overreaction, forgive your parent, make peace with yourself.

If you have a deep and clear understanding that a certain pattern of behavior is not about you, then you are able to separate and make choices that are your own. You are free. You no longer see your child as a "little you" and yourself as the sole reflection of your parent. You can form a new parent/child unit.

CHAPTER THREE

Discipline in
a Virtual World

Now that you have a deeper understanding of your internal parental traps, let's get down to business. Out-of-control, entitled attitudes need strong guidance. So get ready to discipline.

Entitled attitudes begin when parents do not set boundaries and allow their children to "rule the roost." Parents can be fearful of taking control; of giving consequences, punishment, and earned rewards; and of following through on these measures. Too many parents want their children's approval and are afraid children will act out or reject them—as a consequence, parents will often tolerate inappropriate behavior in order to get attention from their children. It is time to take control of your parenting and learn to say no!

Parents don't want to be seen as the bad guys. The parental desire to befriend a child creates huge problems over time and can lead to bratty behavior. Recently at the grocery store, I watched a mother allow her six-year-old to throw green beans down the aisle like they were bowling balls. The beans fell on the shoppers, the floor, the food, and when one landed in the mother's face, she casually said, "Stop it," to her son. This exchange went on five times! The mother was engaged in a cell phone conversation discussing her dinner party for that night. Finally, a woman shopper slipped on the beans and nearly went sprawling head first. The little boy laughed.

"Don't you dare throw those beans. Do you understand?" snapped the woman who fell. The boy started to cry, and his mother was aghast. She growled back at the woman and warned her not to talk to her son that way or she would call the police. The woman went limping down the aisle and said, "You should discipline your son before someone really hurts themselves." The boy continued with his bean bowling without consequences.

Today, a parent often comes to her child's aid and defense—even if the child is wrong. The idea that someone would chastise your precious child is unthinkable. But there was a time when grandparents, aunts, uncles, and babysitters could and would discipline a naughty child without the worry of being politically correct. Children were not allowed to run rampant, and the rules for a child's behavior were clear cut. Children had boundaries and knew what they were. Parents instilled a fear of crossing the invisible line if the child used backtalk, hit, displayed poor manners, whined, or acted spoiled.

Rules are vital to establish respect and harmony in the home. It is important that parents delay gratification and hold their children accountable. A child's demands cannot always be met—nor should they. Parents should stay hypervigilant to children's actions. Clear-cut boundaries need to be set at an early age (before three years old) or by the time a child has verbal and cognitive understanding—and expanded and changed as the child grows.

The key word here is *expectation*. That will be a word emphasized again throughout this book as the main concept in child entitlement. When we fail to set rules and boundaries, a child has no expectations. He will continue to push because he knows that he can. There are no real consequences for his bad behavior. A child will continually act out until the parent loses it or yells.

There has to be clear-cut punishment for negative behavior. A parent cannot wait until her child does something really horrible. You must discipline him the minute he breaks your house rules and you must do so on a consistent basis.

If a child *understands* the rules and *knows* he will be punished when he breaks them, he will feel more secure. Children crave limits. Rules give structure and calm, and help to build strong parent/child interaction in the home. This interaction is what leads to respect, and respect is what leads to a less self-indulged child.

Saying no is the first step toward effective parenting and a better behaved child. Because we live in a world of immediate responses, we expect parenting to be the same. Quick results in one day are not what parenting promises. It is a collaborative process. That means:

- Consistency.
- Open discussions regarding proper discipline.
- Being fair and not giving answers to your child until you have thought them through.
- Not yelling—instead, talk.

When saying, no, remember to:

- Say "no" firmly.
- Say no, and do not change your mind.
- Say no, and realize you are being a good parent.
- Say no, or run the risk of raising a bratty, self-indulgent, entitled child.
- Say no, and stay with it.

The worst thing that will happen is that your child will:

- Say "I hate you."
- Say "You are a bad mommy or daddy."
- Have a tantrum.
- Cry.

The best thing that can happen is:

- Your child calms down.
- Your child breaks rules less often because she knows her limits.

• Your child starts to show more respect for you, your home, and people and things outside of the home.

KNOW YOUR LIMIT

Consider the limits and privileges that you and your child seem to be spending time talking about. What are the limits your child seems to want to push and test? Which of these limits/privileges are nonnegotiable, bottom-line limits, and which are you willing to negotiate? Explore these limits in the following chart:

My Line in the Sand	Let's Talk
List five limits that you are not willing to negotiate or budge on at this time.	List five privileges that your child does not now have but on which you'd be willing to negotiate.
1)	1)
2)	2)
3)	3)
4)	4)

My Line in the Sand	Let's Talk
5)	5)

THE DICTATOR EFFECT

Raising children takes courage. It is an enormous responsibility to shape another human being and can be a most complex and challenging job. The psychological pendulum has swung since our grandparents said, "Children should be seen and not heard." Now, the child voice is loud, it's clear, *and* it's often inappropriate and rude.

Up until my friend's daughter was twelve, she would put her hands on her hips and bark orders at her parents. When she was a toddler, they thought it was cute, complying with the little dictator. As she got older, not only was it not cute—it was downright obnoxious. Her mother was afraid to upset the demanding girl and ran around in circles to please her child's constant requests.

Clearly, my friend had given up her parental power to her child. Child dictators are bossy and feel entitled to act as they please. Dictators try to instill fear. Many little ones threaten to act up, embarrass, or break down if they don't get their own way.

There are ways to take power away from the dictator, but

you have to be willing to tolerate his rants and raves until he sees you are serious about ending the attitude.

When I was a store recently, I heard a five-year-old say to her mother, "You're stupid and a jerk." The mother laughed. Laughed! Clearly, this was not cute. Perhaps the mother was embarrassed, but most likely she was unwilling to confront and discipline her daughter. At best, the child should have been put on time-out and taken out of the store. The fact that this child felt it was okay to speak to her mother in such a manner was what needed to be addressed. When children have no boundaries with parents, they feel "safe" to say whatever they want.

Recently, on vacation, a father was watching his two girls, ages four and six, at the pool. They whined and complained, "We want to go swimming now." The father tried to explain to the girls that it was too cold. The girls refused to listen. They went on for twenty minutes whining and harassing the father, who eventually gave in and let the girls swim in the chilly pool. When the mother arrived and told the girls to come out of the water, they yelled, "No!" The mother did not demand they leave the pool and let it go without a fight. She seemed intimidated by the girls who told her to "go away." Clearly, the children were in charge.

This was also the case when I was out to dinner and witnessed a preteen boy yelling at his mother demanding she order him a steak. The mother said it was too expensive, but the teen ranted until he got his way. The mom begged him to be quiet and ordered the steak to placate her child.

Although you might think that these are isolated incidences, think again. These types of occurrences are more prevalent than ever before. Children have moved to the foreground, not the background. Parents are afraid to bruise their children's egos or assert proper parental authority.

Because an entitled child often has a low tolerance quotient, she may not know how to express her feelings and, instead, act out by hitting. I have seen many children strike or bite parents when they don't get their own way. This behavior should never be tolerated and does not warrant an early warning. Let your child know that certain behaviors will get an immediate time-out or, for an older child, removal of privileges.

In order to avoid entitled attitudes, prepare your child ahead of time for situations that might cause inappropriate behavior:

- Before you go out, let your child know what behavior is expected.

- Tell him that there will be immediate consequences for bossy behavior.

- Tell your child that hitting or biting will never be tolerated.

- Tell her to count to three and take a deep breath in order to calm down.

By giving your child parameters and clear direction, he will not be so impulsive and display an entitled attitude. The key is consistency and following through with discipline. Call in all the troops with a dictator. Your spouse and you need to agree that when your child gets bossy, you need to stop him in his tracks fast and let him know who really is the boss in the family—you.

Kids feel empowered to take over decisions that should clearly be parent-driven. The child's voice is often a reflection of the parent voice. Children will parrot what their parents say. Moreover, a child has more opportunity to listen. She often hears cell phone conversations, suggestive television ads, inappropriate Internet banter, and frenetic video games. A child is given more information than she can process and, in turn, often does not know how to respond. She is not sophisticated enough to understand the consequences of cause and effect. We attribute a level of maturity to children that they don't possess and are surprised when they act in a manner that is inconsistent or destructive.

Kid power is driven by the attitude of right. When a child has too much power, he is unable to process his actions, the consequences, or the line between right and wrong. Parents need to take charge of discipline and find inner strength.

PARENT POWER

My goal is to empower you to be able to guide your child in a way that preserves your sanity and your child's psyche, and that builds a foundation for you to parent a child without entitled and spoiled attitudes.

It is okay to punish your child. This word has gotten a bad reputation. It is okay to give consequences, to remove privileges, to utilize time-outs, to make your child responsible for her actions. It is okay to not constantly give materialistically (but not in punitive ways that put emphasis on the material instead of human value). Your time and attention, and your ability to stimulate your child's mind and imagination, are the real powers you possess.

In order to see the world in a context that is not "me" driven, it is important to give your child responsibility. Children should be assigned a growing list of daily chores and responsibilities by their parents. Particularly in homes where both parents work, it is essential that children learn to make a contribution by sharing in the responsibility of maintaining their own rooms. Neither praise nor threatening to take away privileges is enough to motivate children to complete these tasks faithfully everyday.

In addition to daily chores and responsibilities, there are certain behavior problems such as answering back, disobedience, temper tantrums, fighting with brothers and sisters, and, in some extreme cases, outright defiance and hostility that simply do not respond to traditional parenting attempts to "reason" with a child.

SETTING UP A POINTS PLUS CHART PROGRAM

In such cases, what is needed is a systematic and proven method of motivating your child to follow your instructions and requests that does not involve nagging, screaming, threatening, yelling, or hitting. A Points Plus Chart is a highly effective method of motivating your child on a daily basis without your having to resort to "negative" discipline to achieve your goals for your children.

This powerful motivation program involves using a home and school behavior chart in combination with a positive (+) and minus (–) points system. The program provides a clear structure for motivating your child to complete daily chores and responsibilities and to think twice about the consequences before acting out, whining, and making demands.

To set up a Points Plus Chart, take the following steps:

• Identify behaviors you want to encourage or stop.

• Write the behaviors on the behavior chart.

• Select age-appropriate consequences.

• Describe the program to your child.

• Post the behavior chart.

• Complete the behavior chart.

• Calculate points.

Let's consider each of these steps in more detail.

Identify Behaviors You
Want to Encourage or Stop

So as not to overwhelm you and your child, it is important to start out by selecting only one or two behaviors you want to change or encourage for the first week. In this way, you both can learn the system and debug it quickly. Select behaviors that should occur daily, such as making the bed, getting ready for school by 7:00 AM, or other daily chores. After the first week, you can add another one or two behaviors you want to encourage. Also, during the first week, add one or two behaviors you want to stop, for example, answering back, bullying, or whining. It is always better to start slowly and then gradually build after you are successful with a few behaviors.

Write the Behaviors on the Behavior Chart

Clearly define what behaviors you want to change, and write them on the behavior chart. Be specific. For example: put away school clothes by 7:00 PM, make bed before leaving for school, stop teasing sister, stop answering back, do what he's told.

Select Age-Appropriate Consequences

It is very easy to determine for your own child age-appropriate consequences to increase desirable behaviors and decrease undesirable behaviors. Simply observe what activities your child likes to do most. For example, watch television, play video games, use her computer, listen to his radio, use the telephone, play with a favorite toy, ride her bike. You can then set up a reinforcement menu whereby your child must *completely* earn these privileges. As an example, each 10+ point equals fifteen minutes of television time after dinner. Or, conversely, each 10- point equals ten minutes to bed earlier that night. Remember, to be effective, no freebie privileges are allowed. If you select after-dinner television time as a privilege to be earned, then *all* television time after dinner must be earned.

For chores and responsibilities, you can use the system of + points and − points. For example, if your child is ready for school by 7:00 AM, he earns a +1 point. Alternatively, if your child is not ready by 7:00 AM, he earns a –1, which is then exchanged that evening for ten minutes to bed earlier. In essence, you are using a self-motivation method whereby your child *has the choice* to either earn a + or – point depending on his behavior.

Describe the Program to Your Child

Before implementing the Points Plus Chart program, it is essential that you sit down with your child and describe it in detail. Tell your child what behaviors will be targeted for change and what the points will be exchanged for. Have your child repeat to you in his own words what you have just described so that you are certain he understands you.

Post the Behavior Chart

Place the behavior chart in a highly visible place, for instance, on the refrigerator door, on the family bulletin board, or on the child's bedroom wall. This "conspicuous accountability" can provide additional motivation for your child, since she will receive praise for a job well done (+ points earned) and be questioned why she lost points (– points).

Complete the Behavior Chart

Each time your child earns a + or – point, be certain to post it on the behavior chart immediately or as soon as possible thereafter. If you cannot do this yourself because of work, then be certain that your child's home-care provider knows the program. Otherwise, there is the very strong possibility that points earned will not be recorded accurately, if at all.

Calculate Points

It is essential to sit down with your child daily and tabulate the number of + and – points earned for the day. Children need *immediate* daily reinforcement for their daily behaviors. To further motivate your child, devise a bonus point system whereby achieving a certain weekly total of + points earns several additional bonus points. For instance, if your child earns a predesignated amount, such as 20 + points, then reward such a high level of accomplishment with a bonus (for example, 3 + points). These bonus points show your child that you really appreciate his good effort! (Don't expect a perfect weekly score. Be flexible, reward a good effort, and your child will ultimately keep a positive attitude toward the point system.)

What's important is that your child learns to be responsible and eventually internalize his sense of responsibility to himself and the family.

Examples of Behaviors to Increase
or Decrease with Points-Exchange Value

Add and subtract points in order to calculate the weekly amount.

- Be ready for school bus at 7:00 AM (+1 point).

- Clean bedroom by 6:00 PM every day (+1 point).

- Do homework by 7:00 PM every day (+2 points).

- Teasing your sister (–1 point).

- Don't answer back the whole day (+2 points).

- Disobedience (–1 point each time).

- Home by 3:30 PM after school (+1 point).

- No fighting all day with brother (+2 points).

Each time your child earns a + point, provide a lot of praise and enthusiasm to socially reinforce the targeted desirable behavior. If the behavior does not increase (or decrease in the case of a targeted undesirable behavior) within two weeks, then determine whether there is an underlying problem.

With all points systems, it is important not to use money as a reward, but instead have the child earn positive recognition with the charts program.

Be certain *never* to take away + points that your child

earns. This will only discourage your child and defeat the purpose of the point system—to create a positive family atmosphere.

When a target behavior is occurring at a level that is satisfactory to you, then you can gradually fade out the point system for that behavior. Continue to give praise and attention for the occurrence of a positive behavior or the nonoccurrence of a negative behavior while giving points only every other day, then twice a week, then at the end of the week, and then not at all. If your praise and attention are not enough to maintain behavior, then reinstitute the chart program for that behavior.

Finally, it is important to point out that the chart program is teaching your child a very important lesson: that her behaviors have both immediate and long-term consequences, both positive (for appropriate behavior) and negative (for inappropriate behavior). Your child's understanding of this link between her behavior and consequences will further help her succeed in planning her immediate and long-term goals, and decrease spoiled, entitled behaviors.

Some parents may be reluctant to use these methods because of the time and effort it takes to implement and use these techniques. Unfortunately, if you do not take the extra time now to use these invaluable techniques, you and your child may pay the consequences later. It is vital that you take hold of these years so that you can give your child every opportunity to grow into a responsible, caring, and giving person.

TOP TWELVE LIST OF
PROACTIVE PARENTING RULES

Disciplining an entitled child is difficult. If you give up your parenting to a child dictator, you will be angry and frustrated. Inevitably you will be unable to parent effectively. Your job is to be involved and firm with your child—who is not your friend. This has been debated, but it is better to be a friendly, benevolent leader than a passive doormat buddy. Your child needs guidance and that means making decisions that your child may not like. But he needs to look to you for structure and safe choices. Use the Proactive Parenting Rules as a guideline; then add your own family rules and keep them posted where you can remind yourself of your most important job—being a parent.

1) Know your bottom line and be clear with your child where you are not willing to bend, and be willing to enforce these rules. Consistency is the key.

2) Set reasonable limits with a willingness to negotiate as your child demonstrates increased maturity and responsibility—not indulged demanding behavior. Do not give in to whiny, bratty, or demanding behavior.

3) Be aware of where your child is and who he is with.

4) Get involved in your child's life—observe interactions and reactions.

5) Keep your child involved in activities that capitalize

on her interests and strengths without getting overly
involved yourself (avoid overidentification).

6) Be responsive when your child is willing to
communicate, and use the communication skills you
will learn in this book.

7) Network with other parents in your child's school
and social network about supervision and activities.
Take charge.

8) Be an involved and proactive parent in your child's
school. Listen to what teachers have to say. Observe
your child's behavior with teachers and students.
Teachers can give you a lot of vital information.
Don't be reactive if you hear "something you don't
like," but be open and willing to hear what the teacher
tells you, and take steps to make changes.

9) Be alert to dramatic shifts or changes in your child's
attitude, behavior, performance, friendships, eating
habits, sleep patterns, and grades.

10) Get to know your child's friends and their parents.

11) Look critically at the behavior you, as a parent, are
modeling. Do you act spoiled, entitled, bossy?

12) Actively counter and monitor destructive and
provocative influences on your child's behavior.

All of these rules will put you on track with your child.

CHAPTER FOUR

Who's in Charge?

Ding! Ding! Ding! This is a wakeup call. Are you listening? Good, because you may not like the message. The media is not a new phenomenon. It is part of our cultural fabric. Television, the Internet, texting, faxes, phone, video games, Skype, magazines, books, MySpace, YouTube, blogs, Facebook, and Twitter are all methods of communication. There is minimal censorship on these information highways, and monitoring what your child sees and hears is not an easy task. Media messages can be in your face or subliminal. There is no doubt that the advertisers want to target younger people. After all, this is the age group that will be putting pressure on their parents to make purchases and eventually will become the adults who spend the money.

MEDIA MESSAGES

The media can send the wrong messages to an impressionable child, and it is up to you to monitor this abundance of information. You have the power to plug your child in and to unplug what is offensive and inappropriate. Children are acquiring information at too young an age. They parrot back what they have seen and heard without full understanding. Part of the parent-entitlement mantra is "I don't have control over the media. I want my child to be as informed as his friends. My child is entitled to have a computer, a television, an iPod, and a DVD player." These ideas take away your power to teach your child lessons. In fact, you are in control of what your child has exposure to. The teaching tools need to start when they are toddlers. Once again, a parent needs to find inner strength to fight—yes, fight—losing her child to the media.

An electronic babysitter is not a substitute for a mom and dad. Your child craves:

- Time
- Attention
- Being read to
- Playing games
- Talking to you
- Playing sports
- Family meals
- Nature walks

Technology, by its nature, doesn't advocate verbal communication. When kids don't talk, they tend to be less gregarious, have more limited communication skills, and begin to lack empathy. How can one be empathetic when you are communicating nonverbally or in virtual space? You are not staring a person in the eye when you use technology—you don't see his face—and are not learning how to read verbal and nonverbal facial cues. The human factor is clearly diminished. The overuse of technology creates less empathetic children who become more self-centered and, therefore, less sensitive to human feelings. The irony is that we are becoming less and less intimate in the age of communication.

Time spent together is the key element of parent/child relationships. Start with family time and add technology slowly and appropriately. Children can actually become addicted to the use of computers. Some children will socially isolate themselves if you don't monitor and limit tech and TV time. How often do you see your tweens sitting side by side texting friends? The art of conversation is becoming antiquated.

You do have choices as to what media your child is exposed. The power of the dial is in your control. Sometimes it is easier to just say yes. Think long term. You have a good eighteen years to make an impact on your child's life.

Here are some basic rules to remember about the use of the media:

- **Set limits.** Limit your children's use of TV, movies, and video and computer games to no more than one hour during school days and two hours on the weekend. Do not let your children watch TV while doing homework. Do not put a TV in your children's bedrooms. Do not put a computer in a young child's bedroom. Children have learned to unlock parent controls, and this can be dangerous territory.

- **Plan what to watch.** Instead of channel surfing, use a program guide and the TV ratings to help you and your children choose which shows to watch. Turn the TV on to watch the program and turn it off when it is over. Become familiar with the shows your children watch.

- **Watch TV with your children.** Do not let teenagers flip to suggestive MTV videos and shows when younger siblings are present. Watch TV with your children and talk about what they see. If your children are very young, they may not be able to tell the difference between a show, a commercial, a cartoon, and real life. Be especially careful of "reality-based" programs. Most of these shows are not appropriate for children and can be too mature and graphic for younger children.

- **Find the message.** Some TV programs show people as stereotypes. If you see this, talk with your children about the real-life roles of women, the elderly, and people of other races. Using TV as a teaching tool, not a babysitter, can be beneficial.

- **Help your children resist commercials.** When your children ask for things they see on TV, explain that the purpose of commercials is to make people want things they may not need. But in order to be fair, do taste testing and look at consumer reports. Make your child proactive in her choice of products, and show her how much money you can save for other family items by buying the less expensive product. Don't spend extra money because your child is being manipulated by the media.

- **Look for quality children's DVDs.** There are many quality DVDs available for children. Check reviews before buying or renting programs or movies. Preview DVDs before you show them to your children. Be clear on the messages you want your children to have.

- **Give other options.** Watching TV can become a habit for your children. Help them find other things to do like playing; reading; learning a hobby, sport, or instrument; doing art; and spending time with family, friends, or neighbors.

- **Lock it up.** Put a child lock on your technology. The power is in your hands.

- **Set a good example.** As a role model, limiting your own TV viewing and choosing programs carefully will help your children do the same.

- **Express your views.** When you like or do not like
  something you see on TV, make yourself heard.
  Stations, networks, and sponsors pay attention to
  your opinions. If you think a commercial is misleading
  or inappropriately targeting children, write down
  the product name and channel, and describe your
  concerns. You are the audience and the buyer.

SELLING THE BODY IMAGE

The media will sell anything, and sex is one of the key subjects. Children are entitled to our love and respect. But when decisions are made regarding sexual mores and body images, then the line has to be drawn. There is no entitlement. You are in charge. Girls are especially becoming sexualized at younger ages. Certainly women's liberation stressed trying to empower women not to act as sexual objects, but the pendulum is slowly swinging back. Images of teen girls gone wild, half-naked photo ops, drunken sprees, breast augmentation, and the ever-present obsession with weight has contributed to neurotic prepubescent girls who worry obsessively about their bodies, their images, and their sexuality. Boys are equally affected by overemphasis on body image. The messages of perfect "abs," muscular bodies, sexy six packs, and male paunchy tummies are strewn across the media with as much emphasis as the female image. Boys are prone to similar body consciousness as girls.

How does this equate with entitlement? The images that are packaged and sold to the public come with a subliminal message of entitlement. There is a marketing strategy that sells images of an indulgent lifestyle to children of all ages. The message is that you deserve to have all of the wonderful material objects and will get them if you are thin and pretty. Kids are being sold the message that what they buy and what is popular is what they should be.

The media has played havoc with children's body images. As a result, young people, especially girls, are preoccupied at an early age with their body. The not-so-subliminal message is "You are entitled to have a perfect body, and if you don't, something is wrong with you." Tabloids splash headlines that can send an insecure child reeling: "Jessica, Up Ten, Down Two. How Will Her Career Survive?" "Oprah, Her Struggle to Lose Weight." "Britney, Embarrassed to Be in a Bikini." "The Best Bodies in America. You Can Have One Too." "He Left Her for a Thinner Girl." It is impossible for a young person not to be affected by the constant barrage of information, which creates insecurities in children whose sense of self is just forming. Girls and some boys are constantly dieting and see themselves as "too fat."

The tabloid media feeds into the sense of entitlement by holding up a vision of a "perfect ten." No one can live up to these images. You see young women on reality shows declaring, "I'm gorgeous, so I deserve to win, to be a model, to get the guy, to be the top." On one show, a girl was told she couldn't be fixed up on a date because she was ten pounds overweight. She didn't meet the standards of our body-obsessed society. The message was she wasn't entitled to get the guy. A sense of entitlement is attached to this message that is not healthy. Sexy is being sold in money-making quantities, and a normal, healthy body is considered too big.

These are the subliminal negative messages you want to decondition. Let your children know that these messages have nothing to do with their worth as people:

- The value of a person is measured by her looks.

- You should be thin in order to be pretty.

- You will only attract a mate if you are a certain body size.

- Your physical talents take precedence over your intelligence.

- You must look and act according to media-driven opinion to be accepted.

- You should be sexy. You should be macho.

When children are younger, make sure you follow these guidelines:

- Don't obsess over meals. If your child is not hungry,

don't force him to eat. Ask your child to take a few bites of different types of food. Children will eat what their bodies need.

- Don't discuss your child's weight or obsess if she gains a few pounds.

- Get your child involved in some type of sport or physical activity.

- Children's bodies go through physical changes. Become familiar with their normal phases. Prepubescent tweens can be too skinny or chubby. This normalizes as your child grows and begins adolescence.

- Watch to see if your child eats when he is nervous, fearful, or bored. Get him to talk about his feelings and find activities, like a hobby, to replace food.

- Emphasize personality over pretty, healthy over thin, and self-confidence over self-critical.

MODEL ROLE MODELS

There is a bottom line about entitled behavior, and it involves you. You are the first, best, and most important teacher and role model your child will ever have. Your child is the imprint of you. She looks to you for guidance and information, watching what you do; how you act; what you eat, watch, and listen to; how you dress, treat people, handle money; and what you value. If this seems like a huge responsibility, it is. As she grows, a child is influenced by her peer group, but if strong core values are instilled, she can make it through to adulthood intact. She has a familial base that she can draw upon. Entitled attitudes are often unwittingly instilled in the guise of good intentions, but nonetheless, modeled by a parent who may be self-indulgent, overly competitive, or plagued by feelings of deprivation. You are your child's first line of defense.

Babies bond and imprint the mother as the first role model. Slowly children model both parents. They hear and see more than we realize. Kids are sensitive to their surroundings and will take on the attitudes of their parents.

The key is to be aware. Be vigilant. Be a good role model.

CHAPTER FIVE

Compete Me

Competition is the fuel for entitled behavior. Not to say that competition is bad; on the contrary, it helps children rise to a personal best, gives us goals, and keeps a society working hard. However, the entitled child feels that he should "win" everything, that losing diminishes him, and that winning means crushing the opponent.

Winning is the mantra of our society. How one wins and loses is important for raising an internally satisfied child. A loss should not be viewed as shameful but rather an opportunity for learning. A loss teaches humility; a loss teaches tolerance; a loss teaches about limitations. It pushes you further and allows you to let go of fears. A loss keeps a child focused on the task and concentrates energy on learning more thoroughly. A loss gives a child a chance to try new experiences without the pressure to be the first, the best, the top. A loss teaches the exhilaration of winning when it happens.

For some parents who spend thousands of dollars a year to keep their children in sports gear, personal home equipment, and training camps, a loss is intolerable. Now if you think this

is only about sports, think again. There's also beauty and modeling, academic pursuits, singing and music, computer, cooking, horseback riding, and other innumerable ways to elevate
your child. Many parents are going into debt for the quest to
win, as winning comes at a high price.

According to Florida basketball coach Jordan Adair in a
2008 interview in *Smart Money*, when he sees fourth graders
wearing expensive uniforms and sleeping in fancy hotels, he
thinks, "Where do they go from here? It's setting them up for
a letdown." There is so much push to see children compete at
a high stakes level that some parents have gone into debt to
finance their child's games. The average cost of a high-end
baseball bat can run $300 to $400. Sports camps can range
from $2,000 to $5,000 per week. All of this "stuff" and training can create a child who feels both pressured and entitled.

A lot of this push comes from the parental desire to have a
child nab a college scholarship. But this quest is difficult since
only 2 percent of high school seniors get a scholarship. Parents
may truly believe their child is entitled to a scholarship because
perhaps she was the "top" at her school, but once a child gets
out into the real world on her own, and competes with others
who may outshine her, the harsh reality sets in—she may not
be entitled to win because she is not the best. Parents who
have invested time and money and energy into creating a super
child have a difficult time coming to terms with the idea that
their child may not get everything she wants.

How one wins is equally as important. Win with grace. Win, not at all costs, but to achieve a personal best. Win with fairness. Win for yourself. Win to learn the value of hard work and setting goals. Win, not to crush your opponent, but to elevate yourself.

Competition can lead to a feeling of entitlement if you don't teach your child how to compete. You see the competition push every weekend on the soccer and baseball fields, parents screaming at their children, deriding coaches, and yelling at other players. Ten-year-old Josh, a talented soccer player, was devastated when his father ran onto the field and shoved his coach after a questionable play. Josh wanted to quit playing and lost his desire to have fun at the games. He shut down emotionally each time his dad screamed at him for not getting a hit.

Ironically, this type of behavior is not uncommon. By pushing children to compete aggressively as opposed to assertively, children can become burned out, angry, and overprogrammed, especially if they are trying to please you—the parent. Children need to compete in a healthy positive way, and they need you to be a guide and mentor, not a competitor or pusher.

Tweens are especially vulnerable to competition. They are influenced by strong peer pressure because they so want to be accepted by the group. Therefore, the competition to have the best body and cutest clothes, and to be the best athlete and most popular is fierce. Many parents, in an effort to compete alongside their child, are willing to indulge the bad behavior of unhealthy competition. This poor role modeling is mirrored by impressionable children.

An example of this is Shannon, a fourteen-year-old, whose mother, Joyce, was determined to compete with Shannon's friends' parents in the race for "who has the most expensive" item. Joyce bought Shannon an expensive watch. Her friend's mother, Arlene, then bought her daughter a more expensive watch. Then Joyce bought the latest and greatest Apple computer. Another friend's mom, Sue, bought her daughter an even better one. Needless to say, the material wars could not be won. This competition is an empty one because it teaches children misplaced values and places emphasis on things, not people.

Competition spills over into many areas, especially sports. A child's emotional growth is based on his ability to make choices and then learn from any mistakes that arise from his choices. When a parent constantly intercedes in this process, the child feels insecure, uncertain of his actions. In sports, coaches, too, can push a child too hard. The child's self-esteem can break down, and the child can begin to question his ability. A marginally talented child can pay a huge price when he feels he is letting down his family, coach, and school.

There are two types of competition that can feed into entitlement attitudes. Destructive competition involves a person trying to eliminate his opponent and destroy him. This premise is based on the end goal of winning at all costs. A child who practices destructive competition sees himself not as a team member, but as an individual, above other children. When parents push for their child to be the star, they can create a bully and an egotistical child, a child who feels entitled to win.

Conversely, constructive competition advocates using the opponent to get inspired rather than seeing her as the enemy. Constructive competition emphasizes the child doing the best he is capable of rather than destroying the other person. When constructive competition comes into play, children are able to enjoy benefits including:

- Experiencing peer approval.

- Identifying positively with a group or team.

- Achieving goals as part of a team.

- Sharing common experiences.

- Increasing self-confidence.

REALITY CHECKLIST

To encourage a child to be a healthy, constructive competitor, it is important to make realistic assessments. The following reality checklist will help you to set realistic—as opposed to overinflated—expectations:

- What are your child's best qualities? When you assess

your child's qualities, make sure you consider personality traits such as generosity, fairness, and kindness.

- Do you push your child into areas that you like and he doesn't?

- Do you listen to your child? Children will express their feelings if you give them an open forum. Don't discount what your child tells you.

- Set goals that are not out of reach, but attainable. Many parents expect straight As. That is not always possible. Be fair to your child. Set small goals and give positive reinforcement for even the tiniest amount of progress.

- Assess your child's progress and decide if you overestimated her talents.

- Do you respect your child's personal goals and allow him to compete in his own way? Some children will never have the competitive drive that you would like.

- Do you help your child to accept both winning and losing? This is the most important point. Losing with grace and humility is as important as winning. Both create a framework for good character by teaching us to accept the ups and downs of life and then to move forward.

FILL ME UP

Some children cannot get fulfilled no matter how much you give them. It is never enough. Kevin, age seven, would whine and cry until he got what he wanted. He wore down his mom who came home from work and admitted she didn't have the energy to fight with Kevin. It was a daily routine. Once her son got his way, he would whine for something else. She ran to the mall to get Kevin a new soccer ball, only to have him get bored with it, toss it away, and then ask for a basketball instead. Clearly, his requests had little to do with need or, in this case, want. What Kevin *needed* was attention. What Kevin *wanted* was to get his mother to react. No matter how much she bought him, Kevin could not fill up that empty space inside of himself.

These unconscious thoughts are driven by spoiled behaviors. When entitlement is mixed with competition, a child may also feel pressure. Again, the unconscious thought process is, "I am special, so I am entitled to win because I am the best." It is sometimes painful to recognize yourself as an entitlement-pusher because we all want our children to be successful. But too much giving and getting can create the opposite effect. You may be pushing toward entitlement if:

- You find yourself talking incessantly and solely about your child and his accomplishments.

- You schedule more than one or two outside activities a week for your child and have little quiet at home time.

- You force your child to participate in activities she has expressed dislike for and then chide her if she doesn't do well.

- You make comparisons between your child and others.

- You overindulge your child in order to compete with others.

- You get angry if your child does not meet your expectations.

The last one is probably most important. If a child falls short of our expectations, we either push harder or make a child feel he isn't good enough. Children especially need to be accepted for who they are, because they are so emotionally vulnerable. Each child has his strengths and weaknesses. No human being is perfect, but every one of us is perfectly wonderful in some way.

The entitled child feels that she doesn't have to live up to expectations because she is above other people. But in truth, this is often a cover for real feelings. What traits make your child who she is? Our society has raised such a high bar for children that those who can't meet these expectations never feel good enough about themselves. That's why it is important to help your child reach for her personal best—not yours or someone's else—but her own.

PERSONAL BEST

Some parents might say, "If you don't have high expectations of my child, then he won't try to do his best." But this theory is faulty. It shortchanges your child whose internal ego structures (his sense of self) are built by supporting, not dictating or pushing, his choices and feelings. Self-esteem is nurtured by helping your child create and support *his* view of himself—not just your view. Strong internal structure can withstand negative input because the child believes he is worthwhile.

Children thrive on belief in their abilities, not entitled expectation. They compete with others because we expect them to—the very nature of grades and scores sets children on a competitive edge. Competition is good. In fact, it can be stimulating if a child can learn to reach her personal best and not fall prey to the unrealistic expectations of others—especially parents.

Empowering a child to be successful means helping the child reach his own potential—not one that is unattainable. Empowering a child means taking the power out of our hands and putting it in his. When a child takes personal responsibility for his work, he begins to own his pride. If the parents' expectations are too high and the parent only accepts "perfection," the child may not even bother to try, believing he is set up to fail.

Mark's dad, Alan, paid thousands of dollars to make sure that his contribution to a private school would assure Mark a spot. Indeed, Mark got accepted but, ironically, failed to meet the academic standards set by the school. When the dean suggested that perhaps the curriculum was too difficult for Mark and that he might do better in another school, Alan became enraged. He reminded the dean that he was one of their largest contributors, and Mark was entitled to attend. Of course, the twelve-year-old mirrored his father's attitude and even felt that his poor grades were of no consequence. He believed that monetary contributions in essence, bought his position. Mark had no desire to reach a personal best because he wasn't challenged.

This attitude can set a child up for failure because no matter how much you buy a child, if she does not pursue her interests, personal goals, and wins and losses, she will fall short of not only her dreams, but also, chances are, she will cease to dream at all.

Encourage your child through wins and losses. Part of competition is accepting the outcome and acknowledging that someone else may be superior. Parents should not push a child in an area he is not prepared for. Our society believes you can be anything you want, but in reality this is not true. Some of us *do* have limitations. Be truthful and realistic. Teach your child to prepare, practice, and persevere, and to set goals that are attainable. Be a good role model, and practice what you preach by losing and winning with grace and humility.

CREATIVITY KILLERS

Often, a child who feels entitled will not work up to potential, especially if a parent gives the message "You are special." Many things may stifle children and push them away from their natural inclinations to enjoy learning and the creative process. However learning and enjoying the creative process is important if a child is going to be self-sufficient and capable in her own pursuits.

According to Teresa M. Amabile, Ph.D., a well-known researcher on creativity and author of *Creativity in Context*, some creativity killers include:

- **Surveillance.** Do not hover over children. This makes them feel uncomfortable. If a child is constantly being observed, he is unlikely to take creative chances.

- **Evaluation.** If you judge what a child creates, she is not willing to take risks and will create only to please the parent or teacher.

- **Rewards.** If overused, prizes such as trophies, money, and stars will deprive a child of the intrinsic pleasure of creativity. His goal will be for the prize and not the creative outcome.

- **Competition.** By placing a child in a win-lose situation, someone will come out on the bottom and surely feel unworthy. Creative rather than competitive pursuits should encourage children to progress at their own pace.

- **Overcontrol.** Telling children how to do things— their schoolwork, play, chores—leaves them feeling disempowered. A child feels fearful that any originality will be wrong.

TROPHIES AND TREATS

"Everybody wins!" So says the generation of entitlers who hand out trophies to every child for winning and losing. Fearful of bruised egos and hurt feelings, the politically correct theory has been to give a prize out merely for participation. But the prize should be the experience. A trophy is not what makes a child a winner, and it certainly is not what stimulates her interest and excitement in an activity. The doing, the struggles, and the accomplishments are the biggest trophies a child will ever get.

But if a trophy is the goal, then giving one to everyone makes it neutral—inconsequential. Children may wonder why they should bother to work hard if everyone gets the same prize. It is difficult to treat all children the same because they are not the same. Every child is different and unique. Some are better artists, better athletes, smarter, prettier, funnier, quirkier. If you do not celebrate these differences, it is a disservice to a child.

No one is entitled to win, and that is the bottom line. Competition will never stop. It is part of who we are. The rules of competition are yours to teach. You have the challenge to direct your child to enjoy the process, not just the product; to stress personality over prettiness; to be one of a team, not the only player.

The Seven Types of Intelligence, based on the book, *7 Kinds of Smart* by Thomas Armstrong, are vitally important because every child—person—learns and approaches the world differently. How we approach the world is measured by a combination of learning styles. Some of these learning styles conflict and some are not compatible. A parent may have a challenging fit with his child because he doesn't understand how his child learns. By telling your child she is good at everything, overindulging, and pushing her in areas in which she is uncomfortable, you miss the opportunity to nurture her positive traits.

Review the list of the Seven Types of Intelligence that follows, and try to discern what traits are your child's and how you can best nurture them:

• **Linguistic** learners like words and languages. They like to read and write.

- **Logical** learners enjoy sequencing ideas and are good at mathematical relationships. They are highly organized and generally good at standardized testing.

- **Spatial** learners are creative with good memories. They are artistic, inventive, and often like architectural tasks.

- **Bodily-kinesthetic** learners are athletic and physical. They use instinct more than logic and may excel in theater.

- **Musical** learners recognize rhythm, pitch, meter, and tone.

- **Interpersonal** learners are gregarious people with good social skills. They communicate well and are usually good at public speaking and oral assignments.

- **Intrapersonal** learners understand their emotions. They are more serious, focused, and introspective. They work well independently.

Remember, the goal is to feel empowered, not entitled; to cooperate, not compete; to create a child who contributes and not just takes. Each of us will compete on some level in different areas. Some children who are multidimensional learners get pressure to be the gifted child, the high achiever. Use these traits as a baseline to understanding, not pressure and competition.

BURNOUT

Some children put undue pressure on themselves, which in turn creates anxiety. Parents with unreal expectations can create a nervous child who acts out to soothe his anxiety. Children who have trouble getting satisfied may be in danger of burnout. Many entitled children cannot feel gratified and constantly are dissatisfied. Unlike adults, a child cannot assess his symptoms. Some things to look for in your child are:

- Change in sleeping patterns.

- Change in eating (over or under).

- Loss of interest in friends or activities.

- Unusual anger, acting out, or regressive introversion.

- Grades dropping in school.

When these symptoms persist for more than a week, it is time to take your child to his pediatrician who may refer you to a therapist.

One mom actually said to me, "How could my child be burning out? I give him everything he wants. I never say no. He has every reason to be happy." As naïve as this may sound, there are parents who truly believe an indulged child is a happy child. Herein lies the point: *things* are not what our children need. Once again, children crave time, attention, and boundaries.

There is a place for competition in our society. Let's face it. Everyone wants to win. But don't let your child pay too high a price for the win.

CHAPTER SIX

A World Outside of "Me"

In many respects, the way you live your life affects how your child lives her life. The way you spend your money, how you share, and how much you indulge your child will give her a sense of your personal values. Every family establishes values based on individual ideals and choices. Much of how you choose to live is determined by you. The choices you make are inevitably important in forming your child's character. The trap comes when you establish values based on other people's choices. You must decide what values are important to you— and what you will compromise on.

VALUES

Values are what form people's lives, what create their core. One parent recalled a moral dilemma that gave her pause. Her ten-year-old daughter, Julie, was staying with a friend's family at their vacation home. It was the last night. The family planned a barbeque at their home. They had dozens of bags of food. The mom cooked chicken, ribs, corn, and coleslaw. The kids decided they didn't want to eat at home but wanted to go for pizza instead. The food was tossed rather than saved, and the parents agreed to take the kids out. Hundreds of dollars of food was discarded. As a parent, what would you have done? Refused to go out? Given the food to the homeless?

Think about the way you handle difficult problems. Think about your own values. Think about your parents and how you followed their examples. This is not to imply that your child always will make what you consider proper choices. Many people need to experiment, stumble, fall, and learn from negative experiences to find out what defines their core values.

Values build on themselves. No one experience or discussion is enough to form your child's total value system. It is also not going to change your beliefs if you make a mistake, an unwise choice that compromises your values. It is more important that your child see you as human and honest, as a person capable of saying, "I'm sorry" or "I made a poor choice." These traits will instill respect and trust in your child.

When I was a teenager, I went out with a young man a few times until my parents discouraged me from seeing him, insisting that his values were "messed up." At first, I was impressed by his sports car and palatial home. This boy used to tell me that his father worshipped money over God, and money is what the boy thought was important. He hated his father for having so much control over his frail psyche. His father made him feel worthless. The boy watched his father lie and cheat in business to build a financial empire.

Many years later, I read in the newspaper about two men who paid to have their parents murdered. One of these men was the boy I had gone out with years earlier. I was not terribly surprised. I remembered how he had valued his Jaguar, his solid gold buttons, his Rolex watch, and his diamond ring. He valued *things*—not people, good character, intelligence, or kindness. When his father cut him and his brother off from the business, they could not survive on their own. He had no internal core, no sense of moral fortitude.

I use this extreme story to illustrate how vital it is to build internal values. Do not get trapped into the worship of things. Studies have been done on what makes people happy. Out of the people polled, the largest percentage expressed that their happiness revolved around children, animals, nature, and being loved.

The following chart will help you to prioritize those things that are important to you. Be honest. There are no right or wrong answers. Then have your child(ren) fill out the chart. The purpose of the chart is to enable you and your family to think about your priorities—your values—and perhaps reassess them.

Values Chart—Parents

What is important to you? List in order of priority.

1) _____

2) _____

3) _____

4) _____

5) _____

6) _____

7) _____

8) _____

9) _____

10) _____

Values Chart—Child

What is important to you? List in order of priority.

1) _____

2) _____

3) _____

4) _____

5) _____

6) _____

7) _____

8) _____

9) _____

10) _____

Values, morals, manners, and basic respect are the basis for raising an empathetic, sensitive, and caring child who is not spoiled and demanding. But to do this, you have to have the desire to follow through on threats, not placate with rewards, and to show your child that you share and model the values and manners you want him to possess. The goal is to teach your children the difference between what they need and what they want.

RESPECT

Respect is a difficult concept to explain to a child. The best way to teach respect is to give it. Your child will watch the way you treat other people. But you must also treat your child with respect. Respect is not attained by giving a child what she wants. In fact, respect is better achieved by not giving your child's desires priority all the time. You are showing respect for your child by saying no and keeping to your rules. Otherwise, you create a narcissistic being who views the world only in terms of her needs and wants without regard for others.

By letting a child constantly have his way and not setting strong boundaries, you create an atmosphere of permissiveness and trouble. It is unrealistic to think your child will behave because he intuitively knows right from wrong. A child needs to see that the world does not revolve around him. If a child is not given everything he wants, he learns to accept disappointments without a serious breakdown as he grows older. He gains coping skills, which are imperative to deal with life's stresses and strains. He also learns to respect the people he has to deal with in solving life's dilemmas; if taught otherwise, he will have an unrealistic expectation that people are supposed to do things for him.

This was the case for thirty-year-old Kim. She grew up in a home where everything was done for her and it was forbidden to talk about anything negative. As a result, Kim had a skewed view of the world. She was not self-sufficient as she became a young adult, and she was overwhelmed by many of the minor problems that face all young people. Everything was an ordeal and a trauma. Kim did not have the skills to cope with day-to-day problems. Eventually, she went into therapy because of her anger and low frustration level toward people. She didn't respect rules and regulations. She felt they didn't apply to her. Kim needed to attend special classes to learn how to become an adult and work through ordinary life situations.

In advocating respect, it is important that you respect your own child. I am extremely patient and attentive when my friends have something to say, yet I often don't have the patience to listen to what my child is saying. I do this because I am preoccupied. One day my daughter blurted out, "You tell me to respect what you say, but *you* don't respect what *I* say!" She was right. I discounted the importance of what she said. You must respect your child's thoughts and ideas. You need to give her the same amount of courtesy that you would give a stranger or friend.

A teacher of eight-year-old Devon sent home a note saying Devon's attitude toward teachers and coaches was disrespectful. Although Devon's parents were horrified, it was not so surprising that Devon misbehaved. Devon's father continually yelled and cursed at people in their cars, and Devon's mom was rude to and demanding of salespeople. Since Devon's parents were his primary role models, he acted toward others the way his parents did. Even though his parents stressed good manners and behaving well in school, Devon was more influenced by what he saw than by what he was told. You cannot tell a child, "Do as I say, not as I do" and expect him to comply. The behavior you model is the strongest teacher your child has.

Respect involves:

- Creating high standards of behavior for your entire family. Use the Values Chart earlier in this chapter to help you create a family list.

- Following through on important tasks, even if you think they are unpleasant. This builds character and a work ethic.

- Showing respectful behavior toward your child and others.

- Helping your child to solve problems through difficult times. Coping is a key component in learning to get through life.

To teach values, it is important not to get caught up in the trap of give me, get me, buy me.

THE BRIBERY TRAP

How much is an A worth, or a touchdown, or a clean room? We live in a world that perpetuates the idea that everything has a price. Only give small rewards in order to change or teach a behavior using the Points Plus charts. We see price tags attached to sports figures and celebrities. Children get messages that everything should be paid for. But when you start putting a price tag on your child's performance, you are setting up a bribe. You are stripping him of self-motivation, and by doing this you are taking some of his pleasure away—his pleasure in learning for learning's sake, in being part of a team, in being part of a family.

A lot of giving comes from parental guilt. This is especially true for a working parent who can't spend as much time with her child as she would like. So she gives money and toys as a way to assuage her guilt.

In Jan's case, the toys she bought only created more anger in her six-year-old son, Richard. He cried and screamed when Jan left for work, so she brought home a toy. Richard would grab the toy but later destroy it. It was his way of lashing out, of saying, "Forget the toy. Give me ten more minutes in the morning. Play with me when you get home." Jan eventually rearranged her schedule to spend more time with her son.

How many times do you think you have offered a toy or monetary reward to your child? Five times, twenty times, a hundred times? Bribery is one of the biggest entitlement traps. Many parents think that by offering gifts, material or monetary, a child will comply. But bribery becomes a vicious circle. Yes, the child *might* comply initially. But this quickly changes. Usually the more you give, the more your child wants. Any internal motivation to achieve or behave is squashed. And when is enough enough? What if you want your child to read a book every week and you offer one dollar? Let's say he reads two books. Then he'll want two dollars. What if he reads ten? You can stop at one dollar, but he won't want to read more than one book. He becomes so focused on obtaining money for reading that the pleasure of reading for itself is lost. Bribes become like games. There is no desire to do anything beyond what the bribe demands. You are actually hurting your child's ability to learn because you're demonstrating that learning has no intrinsic rewards.

Gifts or special days out are wonderful and should not be discouraged. But they should not be attached to anything else that sends the message, "If you do this, I'll give you that." Remember, what your child really wants from you is *time*. Most children do not have the cognitive ability to ask for your time and attention. So a child whines and cries. To placate him, you give a reward, a bribe. You are basically rewarding inappropriate behavior and reinforcing negative attention.

There is a fine line between spoiling and meeting a child's needs. Every parent defines spoiling differently, often based on how much a child is given. But spoiling is not based only on giving a child material objects. The attitude with which your child gives and receives determines more about whether she is spoiled. The attitude you display regarding material objects helps keep your child from being spoiled.

Being spoiled is not necessarily equated with how much money you have. Think about the Kennedy children. Probably the last thing you would say about them is that they are spoiled. The family certainly has enough financial means and celebrity status to give their children everything they want, but they place value on education, family, community, and political involvement.

A parent often gets trapped by his own feelings of emotional deprivation and wants to shower his child with everything he feels he didn't get as a child. You might tend to overindulge your child and then expect some overwhelming gratitude. If you don't get it, you become angry and disappointed. You think, "Why is my child so ungrateful for everything I do and give?" You then get trapped deeper by wondering, "Did I give enough?" So you give more, further creating what appears to be a spoiled child who wants more and more. But you have conditioned your child to keep wanting. When you stop giving, the child feels suddenly cut off and confused. So she becomes demanding. After all, she is used to a certain way of being treated, a certain attitude.

THE NET

It takes vigilance not to get caught up in the material net when it comes to your child. We live in a world of things. Try to walk through a mall without having your child beg you for the latest and the greatest. *No* becomes a difficult word when your child is whining, "But all my friends have these." You would think that a simple answer like "I can't afford it" would be enough. But often it isn't, and many parents say that they go without things for themselves to give their children the extras they want.

Other parents, who have no financial restraints, have a no-holds-barred attitude. Whatever the child wants, he can have. One father says, "I've worked to become successful. Why not give my child the things I can afford. Why deny him anything?"

When you spoil or overindulge a child, you create a number of negative entitlement traps that a child will fall into. See if you recognize any of these patterns:

- **Entitlement.** Without a sense of values, a child can start to feel that she is entitled to live a certain way and become overly focused on her own needs. She begins to always put herself first.

- **No sense of value.** When a child is constantly overindulged, he does not appreciate the value, both monetary and not, of what he receives. He can become ego-oriented and selfish.

- **Goals are irrelevant.** A child who is overindulged and gets things without working for them feels no sense of accomplishment and true self-worth. She just wants to get or get it done, and has no sense of pride about doing things for herself. This disempowers a child, and eventually she loses motivation.

- **"If you loved me. . . . "** This trap is a big one. The child uses guilt to get what he wants, and many parents fall right in. For instance, your child whines, "If you loved me, you'd buy that for me. I'm the *only* kid without one." You kill yourself to buy what your child wants, only to have him ask next week for another item he *has* to have.

It is best to use common sense when staying out of a bribery trap by remembering:

- Buy only what you can afford.

- Offer things that are not tied to something else. Give freely without strings attached.

- Do not give out of a sense of guilt.

- You can reward a good deed once in a while, but don't make the deed dependent on the reward.

- Do not buy something you feel is totally inappropriate just to placate your child.

THE BIG QUESTION

Look in the mirror and ask yourself, "What are my beliefs? How do I want to raise my child? Am I willing to make a change?"

Morality is a hotbed issue that parents usually feel uncomfortable discussing because it has become such a politically correct topic. However, it would be hypocritical if I did not talk about morals and the entitlement phenomenon because the core ideas need to be addressed. Parents may be uncomfortable discussing moral issues because, for the most part, we often don't really think about moral questions. Some parents may leave moral discussions to school or religious leaders. But it is a parental responsibility to discuss what your family's moral philosophy is and what expectations you have of your children. Part of society's free-to-be-me attitude has created a generation of children who are confused about issues of sex, drugs, right and wrong, and general boundaries. If a child believes the world revolves around her, then there is no fear of reprisals. The sense of privilege and entitlement sends the message of invulnerability. If children do not have moral adults to model, there will be problems raising moral children. The lines of ethics have been blurred by greed.

The moral model of the last twenty years has been focused inward. This is not to say that there are not kind, generous and altruistic people—there are. But unfortunately, the people we read about and watch endlessly on television and the Internet are those who set the tone of how we live. They are the greed mongers who have set the worst possible example, an example that your child sees and hears about. What kind of person has no moral conscience?

MORALS AND MANNERS

Developing the big "M and M" (morals and manners) should be considered your most important parenting goal when raising a decent human being. Etiquette has all but disappeared in our kick-back, casual, voyeuristic, "me first" society. This is not meant to be harsh, but rather a truthful observation.

While boarding a plane recently, an older woman was desperately trying to get her roller bag in the overhead. Not less than five young men sat and watched the woman struggle. Another lady and I helped the older woman with her bag. Miffed, I declared, "Are there no gentlemen on board?" The comment fell on deaf ears. Why? Because being a gentleman is no longer valued, praised, and expected of most males. Rarely does one hear "please" and "thank you." Personal comfort takes precedence over giving up a seat or letting someone else in line.

"Give me, get me" has become a societal norm, and children, because they mirror parental and peer actions, take on this same behavior. Part of the lack of manners and morals is due to our overly open, media-driven world. There is no shame—no open fear. I wouldn't have dared to sit down before my parents, walk in front of them, or not say, "Please." If I didn't mind my manners, my dad would give me a look, and I'd start to shake.

Today, children feel bold and entitled to act as they please.

There is a casualness and almost lazy attitude about good manners. People move at such a fast pace and are so disconnected with other humans, that manners have become almost antiquated. We spend such a large amount of time listening to computer-generated voices, emails, and recorded messages that we are losing touch with people. The person-to-person interaction is still key to a healthy society because relationships are what nurture us—emotionally, socially, and intellectually.

Many entitled parents think that they can take their child anywhere. Yes, you can, but there are environments that are not conducive to children and where adults would feel more comfortable without a child present. Entitled parents don't care what other people think or feel, and this is picked up by their children. The message they send to their children is a very selfish one: others don't matter; gratifying your own needs is what matters, even at the expense of common courtesy. I have seen parents screaming at toddlers in fancy restaurants, at R-rated movies, and during weddings. Entitled parents are "rights" activists. They advocate that their child has the right to be with them anywhere. But adults have rights as well, and they have a right to a quiet, stress-free evening.

As Karen Deerwester notes in *The Entitlement-Free Child,* children don't really like having to sit in a stuffy restaurant, listening to adult conversation, eating adult food, and having no place to play. Instead of taking your children to adult venues, consider the following:

- Get a babysitter, and reconnect with your spouse
  or partner.

- Decline the invitation.

- Go to places that are fun for both your child and you.

- Be respectful of other adults. Not everyone feels the
  way you do.

- An invitation does not give you "the right" to bring
  your child, especially if your child's name is not on the
  invitation.

The key to dealing with any of these issues is consideration.
Teach basic manners to young children as soon as they can
walk and talk. Manners and morals make the backbone of a
person. They are human details that create an emotional connection and societal acceptance; they can translate to how we
are perceived in our day-to-day lives and help us and our children form strong inner resources.

Manners are best taught when you ask a child to participate
in an activity. Consider the following ways to encourage good
manners in your children:

- Ask your children to help you set the table, and show
  them where the plates and silverware are placed.

- Plan a special party with your child, and use this as an
  opportunity to teach manners.

- Help your child create thank-you notes and have him send notes when he receives a gift.

- Give + points for please and thank-yous until it is second nature to your child.

When a child is involved in an activity and feels useful, she is more apt to want to learn, feel part of the family, and have an investment in the task.

Many kids today show little respect for elders, family, and adult friends. This mark of respect is what constitutes civility in an individual as well as society. Even in animal societies there is a mannerly respect for the elders and one's place in the societal animal structure. Though they may try to assert a position, younger animals are usually put in their place by their mothers, and the children back down and show reverence for the hierarchy.

Conversely, in our present-day society, many parents allow children to back-talk, walk in front of others, not offer a seat to an adult, and push past others. Children need consequences for rude behavior and impolite responses. If you think that no one is looking at behaviors, think again. Adults who have good manners, polite dispositions, and refined communication skills tend to get better jobs and form better relationships than those who don't. How we are seen by the outside world is important in our ability to feel more confident.

Even teens can learn good manners, but of course, it is best to start when a child is a toddler with a simple request to use "Please and thank you." The first line of defense is to use good manners yourself. Teens are quick to say, "You don't, so I won't." Model the behaviors you want your child to display. Be emphatic about rudeness or disrespect when it occurs. These discretions are non-negotiable and should have consequences. Be clear about the positive benefits of good manners. Try to find role models (sports figures, teen rock stars, friends) who display good manners.

With practice, manners can become second nature to a child. He should be constantly reinforced for good manners (catch them being good) and corrected for rudeness.

When a child says "Give me" and you comply, there is a subliminal message that she is entitled to get what she wants. If you teach your child that there is expected behavior, you are saying, "You act a certain way, and you are more likely to be rewarded." Why is this so important? Because in the real world, your child will not have people running to get her what she wants and doing her bidding. If she does ask for something politely, she will have a better opportunity to get her needs met.

Molly, a prefinancial–bust spoiled teen, went to find a job. Her parents were financially strapped and could not support their lavish lifestyle any longer. Molly went on interviews. When she found a job, she dictated to her employer what she would and would not do. She was impatient with customers and had an attitude of "I don't have to wait on you." She felt put upon if someone asked her a question. Her job ended quickly. Her attitude of entitlement was preventing her from moving forward.

The rules of respect are reflected in the manners we teach our children. They go hand in hand, and an ill-mannered child is in essence showing disrespect. If you start when your children are toddlers, you will have the best chance of having them be well-mannered into adulthood.

The following is a Manners 101 chart. You will want to add your own words, behaviors, and etiquette to the list. This is meant as a starter kit. Even if your child is older, you can still impart this information. One is never too old to learn, and you should enforce these manners on a daily basis. Consider putting them on your Points Plus Chart to encourage your child to see the importance of good manners.

Manners 101

Winning Words	Basic Behavior	Essential Etiquette
Please	Consideration of others	Using the correct utensils
Thank you	Responsibility	
May I	Do not interrupt when someone is speaking or talking on a phone	Setting a table
You're welcome		Knowing polite introductions
Excuse me	Speak respectfully to elders	Getting up for elders
I'm sorry	Making your bed	
Is it okay	How to treat friends in your home	
Can I help?	Getting up and giving a seat to an adult	
	Opening doors	

CHAPTER SEVEN

The Human ATM
Money, money, money.
Oh my!

Remember when everyone had a piggy bank? Those pennies added up to dollars, and you could actually open a savings account and save your money. It grew and grew.

Money is the engine of entitlement, the symbol of a society's wealth and abundance. Money has come to mean respect, power, success. But the surprise to our generation is that money, so coveted, can be lost like a house of cards. The upper- and middle-class lifestyle of "easy money" has been declining since the millennium. The credit crunch, mismanaged funds, bad loans, and overconsumption have led to a shocking conclusion: you may not be able to have it all.

Robert J. Samuelson noted in his May 2008 *Newsweek* article, "The End of Entitlement," that, according to the Pew Research Center, 70 percent of households now have two or more cars and a similar amount of satellite or cable TVs; 66 percent have high-speed Internet; 42 percent have flat screen TVs; and the numbers are rapidly rising. More students go to college and incur loan debt for ten years or more. Young adult credit card debt is astronomical. We have not set a good financial example for our children, but it is never too late to start. Our relationship to money is translated to our children through us. We often define people by their money, and children pick up on this.

TEACHING YOUR CHILD ABOUT MONEY

In order to teach your child about money, you have to evaluate your own relationship with it. Ask yourself these questions:

- Would you be unhappy without a lot of money?

- Does money make a person powerful?

- Do your children have to have the "best" of everything in order for you to be happy?

- Would you rather pay the gas and electric bill, or buy your child the new electronics game he is begging you for?

- Are you heavily in debt?

- Do you think you deserve to be rich?

- Can a person be successful without being rich?

There are no wrong or right answers. Only you can honestly define your monetary values and the accompanying lessons you want your child to learn.

MONEY VALUES

With the decline in the stock market, mortgage crisis, and bailouts, we all received a reality check—and so did our children. The desire to indulge may not be possible. When my friend, who was short of money, told her eleven-year-old daughter she couldn't buy her a new iPod, the daughter was aghast. Never having been told no before, the child suggested to her mom, "Just use your credit card."

The generation of children who grew up in the prefinancial bust are not used to parents declining their requests for things. Whipping out that magic plastic is akin to money growing on trees, and, until recently, most of us had started to believe it did. The role model standards you set are what your child will follow.

Do you sometimes feel like a human ATM? Your child asks and suddenly the money appears. Saying no to your child has not been the popular response in recent years, but times change, and the value of money is taking on new meaning. That ATM machine is getting clogged. Even if money is not a problem, the message of "easy money" without responsibility is not a good one to send.

The Money Values Chart that follows gives a perspective on what needs to be taught to our children. Have each family member rate each value from 1 to 5 (1 being the least important, 5 the most). Review each member's answers, and use the information as a forum for open discussion about money and values.

Money Values Chart

Rate the value of each element from 1–5
(1 being the least important, 5 the most.)

Name					
Value of money					
Value of work					
Value of family					
Value of friends					
Value of fun					

When it comes to our children, the subliminal message has been spend, not save—buy, don't wait. If you want it, you can have it. When this message becomes integrated into the psyche, we feel entitled to the monetary gains we've become accustomed to. Pulling back the financial reins can feel like a sense of deprivation if the emphasis in our lives has been about things not people, competition not cooperation, elitism not egalitarianism. Money definitely breeds a sense of entitlement if there are no limits to your child's "must haves," like the $600 designer purse and a new car at sixteen. Previous generations have had to work for these objects of desire. Parents wouldn't and couldn't readily provide whatever their children asked for. Adults, like their children, fell prey to a society where easy money contributed to an attitude of give me, get me, buy me. But money isn't as easy any longer, and the bite of not having it all is here.

FINANCIAL LITERACY

There is nothing more important to teach your child than financial literacy. If parents would provide as much information about managing finances as they do everything else, our society might not be in as serious a financial situation. Budgeting, balancing a check book, saving for the future, paying bills (phone, utilities, rent, car payment, insurance), and stock market and banking information should be as important to parenting as any other life lesson you will ever teach. Eighty percent of teens leave college with some type of debt and may be consumed with it for the rest of their lives. Investment services provider Charles Schwab did a survey of teens and found that only 30 percent of the students surveyed said their parents gave them any kind of financial education.

Being intimidated by money does not help to solve problems. From an early age, a child can learn to budget. Have your school-age child set a goal—perhaps to buy a toy. Have him save extra change. By seeing how much change it takes to buy a toy, your child can get an idea that money is not an easy commodity to obtain.

When I was growing up, money was not discussed, especially because I was a female. There was this unspoken idea that girls didn't need to know about money because they would be taken care of. I was so frightened of money that I was unable to find my own financial power. The female relationship to money has changed as women have become more economically self-sufficient, but many girls continue to be of the mindset that they will be taken care of and that effective money skills can be taken for granted. In addition to this disservice we do our young girls, most children are so used to seeing money as ever-present in the form of credit cards and goods, that the tangible reality of cash is not real to today's generation. By educating your child, you are giving your child freedom. When you understand how something works, you are able to take charge of your destiny. But by remaining clueless, you are fearful and unable to make informed decisions, and you give your life over to others.

Many of us, including myself, have had to rethink, reevaluate, and renew our relationship to money. In doing so, we have had to spread this message to our children—the same children we may have overindulged and spoiled. The only way to begin a new family plan is to be honest with your child.

Consider these ideas:

• Be honest without causing panic about the realities of
  your family's economic situation.

- Start a savings program using a piggy bank or, for older kids, a bank account.

- Have your older children open a checking account, and learn how to balance a checkbook and bank online.

- Limit activities that cost money, and encourage friends to come to each others' homes.

- Use creative methods of play, like cooking, arts and crafts, games, imaginary play.

- Give an allowance, and show your child how to budget.

- Encourage giving. Once a month have your child give something to charity: time, pennies saved, used clothing, books, or toys.

SPENDING AND SAVINGS

In the HBO series, *Kids + Money*, the message is clear: the relationship children have with money is not healthy, and the driving force behind it all is their parents. There is a learned behavior behind spending habits. This is not blame. It is societal misdirection, and believe me, I've been there, done that, and paid the price of raising an entitled child.

Parents who spend untold amounts to make their children happy and, in turn, "keep up with the Joneses," can no longer do so because the money is not available. Children who were used to a certain lifestyle feel deprived and angry at parents who deny them their "due."

The psychology of spending is tied to power and expectation. Parents have the power to spend and set up their children's expectations. Children do not understand the concept of money. It is learned by modeling parental actions.

Alexis, thirteen, was a product of an overspending mother who would use money as a bargaining tool. She spent lavishly on Alexis, who was caught up in the excitement of lavish shopping sprees. Her mom would go into debt and then chastise Alexis when she asked for expensive items and money was no longer accessible. Alexis wanted to continue the spree, but the cash and credit were cut off. Her mom went into poverty mode until the next wave of money started flowing again. This unhealthy financial pattern was adopted by Alexis who, as a teen, was baffled about how to handle money.

The desire to give to your child at the expense of family bills is irresponsible. The material objects are a temporary high that dissipates quickly when the bank account is empty. You can't live in Saks Fifth Avenue and eat Nikes. A BMW will not pay the rent.

ALLOWANCE

Ten-year-old Sasha was asked by her teacher how much of an allowance she received. Sasha announced that she didn't need an allowance because she got whatever she wanted. Clearly, the value of money had no meaning to Sasha. This beginning to her financial planning was not a good start.

In order to teach your child to handle credit, bills, plan, and save, it is a good idea to start with an allowance. This can begin before the child starts school. An allowance gives perspective on what things cost. It teaches responsibility, sharing, saving, and a work ethic.

For a preschooler a piggy bank is a perfect start. You can show her the numbers on bills and even show what a dollar buys. Once a child goes to grade school, you can explain in more detail the nuances of credit cards. Teenagers, the largest consumer population, need to open a checking account, set financial goals, and begin saving.

Additionally, perhaps the message needs to include the fact that no one is entitled to an allowance. Some children view an allowance as easy money to use as they choose without any responsibility, and when the money is gone, there will be more. You have an opportunity to teach your child how to spend, save, and give money—lessons that can serve him well as an adult.

Real Simple magazine (September 2008) polled readers and asked how much of an allowance one should give a child on a weekly basis. The percentages can serve as a guide when you determine your child's allowance:

Children 5 and under	77.5 percent: No allowance
(Use of piggy bank and save change)	20 percent: $1 to $5
Children 6 to 13	30 percent: $1 to $5
	25 percent: $6 to $10
Children 14 to 18	21 percent: $16 plus
	14 percent: $6 to $10

Janet Nusbaum, who wrote *Mom, Can I Help Around the House?*, conducted a survey of 350 parents to find out how many of them expect their children to do chores and help around the house. Only 11 percent of the parents polled said their children contributed toward the household. By creating an allowance and reward structure, you are motivating your child to be more proactive in helping with chores, setting goals, and creating a work ethic.

An allowance is also an excellent way to teach children money management and how to budget for long-term goals. If your child wants a certain toy, help her to understand how long she will have to save to get that toy. If you have a teenager, have him pay a portion of his car insurance or have him pay for his own gas. The old saying, "Learn the value of a dollar" has never been so relevant. Children have no connection to what money can buy. When children have to participate (no matter how small the amount), they get not just knowledge but appreciation.

THE CHARITABLE CHILD

Giving is getting if you teach your child to be charitable. This does not have to be just a money issue, because charity involves so many other aspects. But giving is the best way to decrease Give Me, Get Me, Buy Me attitudes.

There are so many ways to give back to your community and beyond. You can start when your children are in preschool. From the time my daughter was five years old, we would spend Thanksgiving serving a dinner to those less fortunate. As she got older, she would help write letters for homeless people to their families. She recalled recently that these experiences have stayed with her. I can truthfully say she is a giving human being and has taken these lessons into adulthood.

Consider implementing the following ideas for giving within your own family:

- **Personal giving box.** Gather clothes and toys that your child outgrows. Leave the box in a place where your child can see it and have her donate on a regular basis.

- **Food drive.** When you go to the store, buy extra—even if it is a few cans of food—and have your child put it in a donation box to take to the charity of your choice.

- **Favorite charity.** Encourage your child to find a charity of his choice. This could be anything from saving an endangered species, being a pen pal with a soldier, building homes for Habitat for Humanity, cleaning up the beaches, planting trees, or helping the environment. Participate with your child and make charitable giving part of your family plan.

CHAPTER EIGHT

We Are Family

Our interpersonal communication skills are slowly disappearing. It is estimated most kids today text each other 400 percent more than just five years ago. There is no voice, no in-person intonation. Shorthand communication creates shorthand thinking. The brain is not challenged when everything is provided by electronic messaging. Once again, a child is not entitled to own every media device invented, and she is certainly not entitled to use them at her whim.

This is where parents need to draw the invisible line. There should be strict rules regarding the use of cell phones, computers, and other electronics. One family I spoke with e-mailed each other from room to room. The siblings would text one another, and the parents would e-mail to their kid's computer. They could have gone weeks without actually hearing a voice.

"TALK TO ME"—COMMUNICATE

If you want to have a child who is not bratty and disassociated, then talk to him. You can't develop a relationship with a machine. Children need closeness: eye contact, the sound of a parent's voice, a touch, smile, verbal cues. Parent-child communication is vital to a healthy relationship but often overlooked as a given. As children become adolescents, communication breaks down further. Often, without realizing it, you do most of the talking, and your child does the listening—if he hasn't already tuned you out. In past generations, there was a parental dictatorship. I wouldn't have ever considered arguing or questioning my parents' directives. The entitled child has turned the communication channel upside down—she gives the orders and instructions; the parents listen.

There are so many complicated challenges in our lives today that communication skills are needed to talk about sensitive societal and family issues. Parents need to be able to handle negative emotions that can accompany growing up. Open communication allows a parent to pick up on a child's feelings about the pressures of school, sports, and societal interactions. Also, by listening to your child, you will be able to determine what activities he has an interest in and perhaps talk honestly about his thoughts and feelings.

One of the most difficult things to accomplish is good communication with an adolescent child. Every issue seems to press hot buttons. The most benign question can be met with raised voices and temperamental outbursts. Teens are under such enormous pressure from academics, social expectations, and sports that the added pressure may cause an adolescent to shut you out.

When Ron asked his thirteen-year-old son, Ray, to do something, he was met with, "In a minute." The minute never came for Ray, and he rarely would listen to his father's requests. Ron would lose his temper at Ray's retort, since he knew it was meaningless. This dialogue became a negative pattern that repeated itself again and again. Ron yelled, and Ray tuned him out. They didn't have the communication tools to begin a productive dialogue. As a result, Ron and Ray just kept on fighting and growing more distant every day.

Ron isn't the only parent who gets frustrated by a lack of communication and turns to anger. When Nancy's ten-year-old son didn't listen to her, she yelled at him, "Trying to talk with you is useless. You never listen. I'm not even going to bother." Nancy constantly criticized her son, and his only defense was to withdraw. Her anger didn't help the communication problem—it only made it worse.

Like many behaviors, communication becomes habitual. The more we fail to talk out our feelings and listen to one another, the more we fail to communicate and often misinterpret words and actions.

FAMILY MEETING

The family meeting is a chance for everyone to join together to discuss family business, feelings, hurts, and happiness, and generally expand the level of overall communication.

There is a structure to the family meeting. It is not a place to whine or attack the other person's vulnerabilities. It is a place to be heard.

Sean, an overindulged ten-year-old, spent ten minutes whining and complaining that he didn't want to talk or go to the family meetings and didn't have to. His parents, so worried about Sean's feelings, allowed the boy to no longer be part of the family meeting on the pretense that "We don't like to force our children to do what they don't want to." Obviously, the purpose of the meeting was lost, and the parents continued to indulge bratty behavior.

To have a productive family meeting, meet as a family once a week (or more during crisis) at a specified time. Set the timer. Everyone gets five minutes to talk out their feelings, ask questions, and express thoughts. The family member can't be interrupted or judged. This is a "free" zone. The goals are to listen, talk, and learn.

LISTEN

Many communication problems occur when people don't hear one another. When emotions are high, it is sometimes difficult to listen to what is really being said. Also, we might not want to hear what someone is saying because we don't like the message.

As parents we must also be careful of the messages we give

our children. A parent who wants something of her child often conveys the message in a punitive or negative manner. Contrary to what some parents think, kids do hear what they say, although many will act indifferent as a defense. Negative verbal messages become inbued. For instance, if you say, "I see you got a C on your test again," your child may hear, "You only got a C. How poor. You'll never do well. You are not very smart." The child may then feel pressured or nagged, and if this message is "heard" repeatedly, it will become ingrained, causing the child to believe that he is indeed stupid.

Alternatively, in an effort to get your child to do better, you may be sending a message that your child hears incorrectly. If a child is told, "You deserve to have the best," what she may hear is, "If you are not the best, you are not okay." The child hears a hidden meaning behind the words. Unfortunately, communication breaks down even more because the child doesn't know how to say, "I just want to be who I am." Instead, the child may withdraw or try even harder, attempting to please her parents at her own emotional expense.

Miscommunication can create hostilities based on wrong assumptions. Use these skills for more effective communication:

- **Do not attack the other person for their choices or ideas.** If your child wants to drop out of soccer to play the guitar, listen to his feelings and reasons. Don't put down his choice because it does not fit your desires.

- **Let the other person complete what she has to say.** Wait a minute before answering if it is a hot topic. Don't interrupt or let your child interrupt. Each person should count to ten before answering.

- **Don't be impulsive.** Think about what you want to communicate and frame your words positively. We tend to lash out at others when they say something contrary to our views. Think about how you would react to what you are going to say. You get further with kind words.

- **Be honest but not hurtful.** Avoiding an issue can create misunderstanding. If your child is not a great athlete, focus on the skills she does best. But don't lie and tell her she has Olympic potential if she works harder.

- **Pay attention and look the person in the eye.** Let the person know you care about what he is saying, and you will communicate better. This skill develops empathy.

- **Stay on the subject.** Don't interrupt with stories about yourself. Let the other person talk about herself and complete her thoughts.

- **Ask informed and caring questions.** If your child is studying Shakespeare, try to get him to teach you something.

- **Don't always give advice and your opinion.** Children are used to adult opinions—nagging, pushing, and advice. Try to develop a give-and-take approach with your conversation. Not every subject calls for our opinion. Children can be extremely insightful. Listen to their advice and opinions.

FAMILY PROBLEM SOLVING

When you have learned to communicate better, you will need skills to help your child (and family) solve problems. Problem-solving tools can encourage cooperation among family members and prevent negative input. During a family meeting, members can brainstorm together to try to find solutions to problems. Try to stay goal-oriented rather than identifying negative behavior. For example, don't talk about your teenage daughter's weight or your son's laziness every time you have a meeting.

Parents often discuss problems at the worst time because they wait until there are strong, angry feelings. If you are upset and you approach your child with angry feelings, she will become defensive or shut down. You want to try and identify and solve problems early on.

The following gives positive ways to initiate such a discussion with your child.

- **Approach your child at an appropriate time,** not when you are both in a hurry, and not in the heat of anger. Busy parents often discipline on the run, and the problem escalates. You don't solve problems when you are upset.

- **Sit down.** Take time without interruptions—phones ringing, appointments, classes. Unplug everything.

- **Decide who should talk to your child.** If you are too combustible, maybe another family member should approach the subject. I'm the designated talker. My husband gets way too upset. Both parents can overwhelm some children.

- **Think about what you want to say.** Don't attack.

- **Do not criticize, scream and yell, or be sarcastic.** These tactics usually get you nowhere. Kids will tune out, cry, scream back, or walk away.

- **Try to be calm and nurturing.** Better yet, try using humor. If you can neutralize a situation with humor, you have a better chance of being heard.

Rules for Problem Solving

The following steps are the basic rules for problem solving. No rules are set in stone, but they can help get you through difficult family situations.

- **Let everyone participate** in defining the problem.

You will be surprised to see that everyone may view a problem differently.

- **Write down all suggested solutions,** without endorsing or negating anyone's ideas. Some way-out suggestions may ultimately turn out to be the answer.

- **Avoid criticism or hostility.** This creates an angry forum. If you do start to argue, everyone take a ten-minute time-out to cool down. There is no right or wrong. It is a collaborative effort—so everyone needs to agree. If you get angry because you only see your side, you have solved nothing.

- Once you and your child have written down all possible solutions, **evaluate the solutions.** Eliminate suggestions that clearly won't work.

- **Find a solution that is fair and agreeable** to everyone. Be willing to compromise. This is the most important point. If your child tells you he doesn't want to play soccer anymore—compromise—see if he would agree to find another activity he likes better.

- **Put your plan into action.** If your solution doesn't work, try an alternative. Be willing to make changes, and go back and reevaluate what's working and what's not.

If you can teach your child these skills, you will be giving her tools she can use her entire life. By working together to be open and fair, solve problems, and release feelings, you turn negativity into positive parenting.

You are now heading toward changing entitled behaviors. Perhaps the finish is the most difficult because it asks you to take the hardest and most realistic look at yourself and then make changes. Change for many of us is difficult. Try to think of the finish as a challenge—a competition, if you must—to become a more effective and thoughtful parent.

All of these tools for communication will help to get you out of a negative frame of mind. When children—and adults—are listened to, they tend to be less reactive, less egocentric, and more empathetic.

Communicative empathy eliminates the need for spoiled, entitled behavior because the value shifts to the internal person and not to what he is and has externally. When we feel close to people, when we are accepted for who we are, when we can express feelings honestly, we are fulfilled.

NO-GUILT ZONE

Guilt! It's an insidious little monster. When I went back to work, I felt like I had done something wrong. Mind you, my daughter was five years old and in school all day, but that did not assuage my feelings of being "not quite a good-enough mommy." That led me to wonder, what is a good-enough mommy?

This was the dilemma for Rachel, a single mother of two children. Nine-year-old Megan and five-year-old Paul learned to play their mom Rachel like a fine-tuned instrument. Rachel worked long hours to help support her children. When she returned from work, the kids would start to whine continually from the minute she walked in the door. She got in the habit of allowing her kids to eat a dessert or get a new toy just to placate their crying and tantrums. Rachel let each child have a television and computer in their rooms and encouraged them to engage in visual activities in an effort to use what Rachel called her electronic babysitter.

This cycle of "give and get" guilt can lead to a child who watches 40,000 commercials a year. Rachel, guilt-ridden that she worked all day and did not spend enough time with her children, felt the need to give and buy to placate her guilt. She allowed her children to define her role as a mom.

Working moms are the key guilt target. The negative cycle of behavior escalates as the economy wanes, and increased numbers of women are looking for work. There are more divorces and single mothers than ever before in history. There is no shame in working. It is important to instill family unity as part of a child's upbringing. Tell your child, "Mom and Dad work in order to help our family. You are part of our family."

The children should not be set apart from their parents. That is what promotes guilt. The thinking is, "I am not here. I am not home enough." It is not about "I." You are all a "we." Make your children responsible. Give them a help list prior to your arrival home from work—perhaps, feed the dog, water the plants, set the table. When your children feel included, they are more apt to think of you as a team, thus fostering cooperation with less acting out and less guilt.

GOING IT ALONE

Single parents especially tend to overindulge out of fear, guilt, and overcompensation. Divorce feeds into parental guilt, control, and depression. A divorce often makes parents feel like failures and affects the relationship with their children.

The reality is that trying to create the nuclear household of past generations is unrealistic. The quality of the interaction among the existing family members is more important than who the members are. A mother and father living harmoniously in one household is wonderful, but this often is not the case.

It is important to recognize any unrealistic expectations you are putting on both yourself and your child in a single-parent household. A child picks up on your internal worries and transfers them to himself. Some parents build up children to feel entitled because they worry something is missing.

When Diane divorced, she became extremely protective of

her children. She saw herself as a caring parent, feeling that she needed to be more watchful of her children now that she was alone. But in reality, she was smothering her eight- and eleven-year-old girls. Her fears of loneliness and having to be responsible for everything herself were transferred onto them. She wouldn't let them have sleepovers, go to camp, or have play dates after school. She wanted the family, without her husband, to be together constantly. The children became both fearful and resentful. They wanted more freedom but were afraid to venture out because of their mother's controlling and overprotective attitude. They began to feel entitled to all of their mother's time and attention. The unspoken subliminal message was that because of the divorce, she owed them her life.

Dave was angry about his divorce. He felt that because his life was so altered, he would indulge his children. His ex-wife felt similarly. They showered the children, not just with material objects, but instilled the attitude that they were entitled to get what they wanted. Both parents operated from a point of guilt and anger.

Divorce can tear into the family structure and destroy the fabric of children's lives. Suddenly what seemed like solid ground collapses underfoot. But the way each parent handles a divorce is the key to keeping your children emotionally healthy. Parents need to stay out of the anger and entitlement traps in front of children.

Some of these traps for divorced parents are:

• Yelling at one another and calling each other names.

• Making hurtful accusations.

• Discussing who will take the children and where they will live.

• Discussing money and how material objects will be distributed.

• Asking a child to choose one parent over the other.

• Buying expensive gifts and not enforcing chores, rules, and limits.

A mother and father need to make a joint effort to do what is in the best interest of their children. This may be difficult, but inevitably it is the only way to raise a centered child in the wake of divorce. Then, as single parents, you both can go on to have a positive relationship with your children.

These are the myths and truths to keep in mind after divorce:

Single-Parent Myths

• In order for a child to be psychologically healthy, she must grow up with a mother and father living at home full time.

- Divorce is what causes all of children's behavior and school problems.

- You must overcompensate for your child to be happy.

- You need to make up for lost love that your child is missing after a divorce by overindulging.

Single-Parent Truths

- Single-parent families are not abnormal; they are as common as nuclear families.

- All children experience some behavior problems when there is a change in the home—whether a move, a new sibling, or a divorce. The problems can be dealt with by being supportive and using communication techniques.

- You don't have to give material objects to assuage the guilt of a divorce.

- Children want stability and love, no matter what the parental relationship.

BLENDED FAMILIES

At least one-third of all children in the United States are expected to live in a stepfamily before they reach age eighteen. This type of family is becoming more of the norm.

Laura, age ten, and Brad, age fourteen, had a mom, a dad, a stepmom, five stepsiblings, and a slew of step grandparents and extended family. But this *Brady Bunch* picture was not what it appeared. Laura and Brad were not happy with the amount of attention they received, and each felt lost in the blended family. Their father was a workaholic who, out of guilt, spoiled the children with constant gifts and indulgences. The stepmom was afraid to set limits because of disapproval from her husband, and the mom wanted to be favored by her children, so further overindulged and spoiled them in order to gain their love and loyalty. This psychological chess game shifted children from one family to another without any core parenting.

The pain and guilt of divorce and remarriage can take its hardest hit on the kids. Each parent feels everything has to be equal, which leads to overindulgence. Many children pick up these signals and play one parent against the other. The children feel entitled because of the parents' guilt. But this only hurts, not helps, a child's ability to cope and adjust to a new familial situation.

No matter what your feelings, your children should not have to get dragged into personal marital conflicts. Extended families can be a blessing in your children's lives if you are willing to put your anger aside for their well-being.

The most important thing to remember is that a blended family takes time—time to develop relationships. How you act and react over time will be the starting point. Overgiving by the primary stepparent will not create a good relationship. This only sets up expectations on the part of the child. Pull back and let feelings unfold naturally. Don't try to push yourself on a stepchild.

The Do's and Don'ts of Blended Families

Do . . .	Don't . . .
. . . reassure children that the divorce/death was not their fault. Invite questions and discussion.	. . . push your children into creating relationships. Allow bonds to evolve slowly and naturally. Give your children the time, space, and flexibility to adjust to the new situation.
. . . start talking with your children about the possibility of blending your family long before your marriage.	. . . expect your stepchildren to call you mom or dad. Let them decide what they want to call you, or mutually select a name that you are comfortable being called.
. . . assure children that they will continue to have a relationship with the non-residential parent.	
. . . begin a dialogue (family meeting) about the future family life, letting everyone acknowledge and mourn losses through an open discussion of feelings.	. . . forget your marriage by focusing exclusively on the family. Make alone time with your spouse consistently

(Continued)

Do . . . *(continued)*	Don't . . . *(continued)*
. . . present a unified parenting approach that is evenly applied to everyone in the family.	and nurture your marital relationship.
. . . spend some time alone with each child and stepchild, connecting one-on-one.	. . . allow conflict to arise between adults in front of the kids.
. . . establish new traditions for the blended family.	. . . hesitate to ask for help from family members, friends, or support groups. Blending two families can be hard!

Divorce makes it hard to set appropriate limits. Giving to a new spouse or stepchildren can create anger and jealousy with your children. But most children, if given love, attention, and boundaries, will recover over time and begin to accept this new extended family.

THE FAMILY DINNER

The family dinner is fast becoming an antiquated occurrence. Mom, Dad, and the kids are busy, whether going from one appointment to the other, or participating in sports activities, dance class, music lessons, tutors, computers, or work.

Dinner is a "grab what you can" time of the day. If you calculate the actual time you spend with your children, for some parents (especially working parents), it is less than three hours a day.

The family dinner *must* become a priority. Even if you are a working parent. Make sure you have at least one night a week that's family dinner time. There has to be a time when children can build memories of the family together. This time creates security and a sense of belonging. Meals are a great buffer between people and a natural time to share conversation. Rituals, like the family dinner, will help your child to see the family as a whole picture. A child is not the special entity—but a contributor of the family unit.

CHAPTER NINE

How to Unspoil

It is never too early or too late to pull back on overindulging your child. After reading this book, hopefully you are motivated to begin. Without judgment, this is a favor to your child and yourself.

HOW TO AVOID SPOILING

According to *Pediatric Advisor*, there are specific ways to avoid spoiling. Consider the following list.

Don't Give Children Presents or Favors

Don't give gifts in order to get your child's love and attention and create a buddy relationship. You're a parent first and a friend second.

Require Cooperation with Important Rules

Don't be afraid to step in and parent.

Your child must respond properly to your directions long before he starts school. Important rules include staying in the car seat, not hitting other children, being ready to leave on time in the morning, going to bed on time, and so forth. These adult decisions are not open to negotiation. Do not give your child a choice when there is none.

Give your child a chance to decide about such things as which cereal to eat, which book to read, which toys to take into the tub, and which clothes to wear. Make sure your child understands the difference between areas in which she has choices and areas in which she does not. Try to limit your important rules to no more than ten, write them down, and be willing to take a firm stand about these rules. Also, be sure all of your child's adult caretakers enforce your rules consistently.

Expect Your Child to Cry

Distinguish between your child's needs and wishes. Needs include relief from pain, hunger, and fear. In these cases, respond to crying immediately. Other crying is harmless and usually relates to your child's wishes, and this is where entitlement begins. Crying is a normal response to change or frustration. When crying is part of a tantrum, ignore it. There are times when you will have to withhold attention and comforting temporarily to help your child learn something. Don't punish your child for crying, call him a crybaby, or tell him he shouldn't cry. Avoid denying him his feelings, but don't be overly moved by his crying. Respond to the extra crying your child does when you are tightening up on the rules by providing extra cuddling and enjoyable activities when he is not crying or having a tantrum.

Do Not Get Sad or Nervous Because Your Child Doesn't Get Her Way

She will survive. I promise! Be strong!

Do Not Allow Tantrums to Work

Children throw temper tantrums to get your attention, wear you down, get you to change your mind, and get their own way. Crying is used to change your no to a yes. Tantrums may include whining, complaining, crying, breath-holding, pounding the floor, shouting, or slamming a door. As long as your child stays in one place and is not too disruptive or in a position to harm himself, you can safely ignore him during a tantrum. By all means, don't give in to tantrums.

Don't Overlook Discipline During Quality Time

If you are a working parent, you will want to spend part of your free time each day with your child. This time needs to be enjoyable but also reality-based. Don't ease up on the rules, take her shopping, buy "things," and call it quality time. If your child misbehaves, remind her of the limits. Even during fun activities, you need to enforce the rules.

Don't Try to Negotiate with Young Children

Don't give away your power as a parent. When your child reaches the age of two or three years, you'll find that she doesn't play by the rules. No toddlers do. Young children mainly understand action, not words. The more democratic a parent is during a child's first two or three years, the more demanding the child tends to become. In general, young children don't know what to do with power. Left to their own devices, they will make constant demands. If they are testing everything at age three, it is a recipe for trouble later on and should be addressed. If you have given away your power, take it back; set new limits and enforce them. You don't have to give a reason for every rule. Sometimes it is just because "that's the rule."

By age four or five, your child will begin to respond to reason about discipline issues. During the elementary school years, show a willingness to discuss the rules. By age fourteen to sixteen, an adolescent can be negotiated with as an adult. You can ask for his input about what limits and consequences are fair (that is, rules become joint decisions). Inevitably, you are the final word.

Teach Your Child to Cope with Boredom

You can provide toys, books, and art supplies. Your child has the choice to use them. Assuming you talk and play with your child several hours a day, you do not need to be her constant playmate. Nor do you need to always provide her with an outside friend. When you're busy, expect your child to amuse herself. Even one-year-olds can keep themselves occupied for fifteen minutes at a time. By age three, most children can entertain themselves about half of the time. Sending you child off to "find something to do" is doing her a favor. Much good creative play, thinking, and daydreaming come from coping with boredom. Consider enrolling your child in a play group or preschool.

Teach Your Child to Wait

Waiting helps children learn to deal with frustration. All adult work carries some degree of frustration. Delaying immediate gratification is something your child must learn gradually, and it takes practice. Don't feel guilty if you have to make your child wait a few minutes now and then (for example, when you are talking with others in person or on the telephone). Waiting doesn't hurt a child as long as it isn't excessive.

Don't Rescue Your Child from Normal Life Challenges

Changes such as moving and starting school are normal life stressors. These are opportunities for learning and problem solving. Always be available and supportive, but don't help your child with situations she can handle by herself. Overall, make your child's life as realistic as she can tolerate for her age, rather than going out of your way to always try to fix every problem. Her coping skills and self-confidence will benefit.

Teach Your Child to Respect the Rights of Adults

A child's needs for love, food, clothing, safety, and security obviously come first. However, your needs are important too. Your child's wishes should come after your needs are met and as time allows. This is especially important for working parents where family time is limited.

Both the quality and quantity of time you spend with your child are important. Quality time is time that is enjoyable, interactive, and focused on your child. Children need some quality time with their parents every day. But spending every free moment of your evenings and weekends with your child is not good for you or your child. You need a balance. Scheduled nights out with your spouse or friends will not only nurture your adult relationships, but also help you to return to parenting with more to give. If your child isn't taught to respect your rights, he may not learn to respect the rights of other adults and children—and that is entitlement.

All of these life skills will help your child with rules and respect. These are the basis for reversing entitled behaviors. It is a good idea to start with a base line by determining your priorities as well as your child's.

DETERMINING YOUR PRIORITIES

As you go over the priority lists, spend time thinking about what really counts in your life. You might be surprised to see how many things you are willing to let go. Your priorities might shift when you decide what is truly important. All of this leads into how to unspoil your child and yourself. You can feel rich without a big bank account or fancy cars and clothes. Just get your priorities straight!

Parental Priority List #1

List the ten things you can't live without:

1) _____

2) _____

3) _____

4) _____

5) _____

6) _____

7) _____

8) _____

9) _____

10) _____

Parental Priority List #2

List the ten things you are willing to give up or change in your life:

1) _____

2) _____

3) _____

4) _____

5) _____

6) _____

7) _____

8) _____

9) _____

10) _____

Child Priority List #1

Ask your child to list the ten things he can't live without:

1) _____

2) _____

3) _____

4) _____

5) _____

6) _____

7) _____

8) _____

9) _____

10) _____

Child Priority List #2

Ask your child to list the ten things she is willing to give up or change in her life:

1) _____

2) _____

3) _____

4) _____

5) _____

6) _____

7) _____

8) _____

9) _____

10) _____

PRAISE AND ENCOURAGEMENT

It is healthier and more productive to be an encouraging rather than an overly indulgent parent. Encouragement helps to create a positive relationship, increases cooperation, and helps your child develop self-confidence and self-reliance. Praise is what a child receives from outward sources—through grades, trophies, or others' opinions of him.

Self-esteem is inner confidence and a feeling of self-worth—"I'm okay." These feelings emanate from unconditional self-acceptance and self-respect. You cannot give your child self-esteem by overgiving or overpraising. But you can perpetuate it by your behavior. Self-esteem builds from within. Self-confidence does not come from what others think about you. It comes from what you think about yourself, and that is why encouragement as opposed to praise helps to create positive self-esteem.

Helping your child to appreciate her good qualities and not dwell on negative traits can instill good self-worth. Teaching her to put her talents to good use can also further her feelings of usefulness in society. Some parents inadvertently give a child negative messages by angry looks, nods of disapproval, constant criticism, and by saying, "You can do even better than Susie or Molly." The child never feels good enough, no matter what she does. When your expectations are always so high, your child may give up because there is too much pressure to perform. However, if you overpraise a child, she may fall apart when she fails. She'll have no inner resources from which to draw.

As a concerned parent, you can learn the difference between praise and encouragement:

Praise	Encouragement
Can help a child learn to view himself from another's perspective.	Focuses on the child assessing his own accomplishments.
Is assessed by grades, rewards, and trophies.	Helps a child accept her efforts, and she develops a desire to learn without rewards attached.
Can lead to a child blaming others when she fails at something because the expectations on her are so high.	Helps a child become willing to make mistakes and start again. A child will become more readily willing to take responsibility for himself.

LET CHILDREN BE CHILDREN

Children want very little. We provide the trappings. But watch a child at play, and you will witness imagination, curiosity, self-reliance, and teamwork. This is children being children. As mentioned numerous times in the book, children are blank slates. We are responsible for early influences. By the time a child is six years old, her personality is fully formed. But the external stimuli are in your control. Take your child to the beach or a park. She needs very few toys or media to make her happy. The strength of nature on a child is extremely powerful. Use nature as a free playground in all of its wonder to teach, inspire, and provide joy to your child. Give time to talk, walk, and explore. Let children climb trees, run barefoot in the sand, make a castle out of twigs, walk in the woods, play in the snow, stand in the rain. Before life bombards them with images and buttons, money and media, let children be children.

EPILOGUE

The strength, balance, and courage it takes to turn around entitled behavior in your child are enormous. But the end result is a more responsible, caring, reasonable, and emotionally healthy child. There will also be more harmony and balance in your home. Because entitled children are so self-focused, the "my needs are to be met first and foremost" attitude can cause anxiety, anger, and arguments within the family. Remember, no matter how much you give or indulge an entitled child, it will never be enough. He can't fill up unless you draw the line—once and for all. After reading *Give Me, Get Me, Buy Me,* your goals should be refocused on how to move out of entitlement and into proactive parenting. These are points to remember when working through your plan.

Perhaps Eckhart Tolle expresses the roots of entitlement best in his book *A New Earth.* He describes our confusion of *having* with *being.* As Tolle says, many of us believe "I have, therefore I am." This message, if transferred to our children, places emphasis on the external and material, not on the value of the individual as he is without anything but his mind, heart, soul, and physical presence. Teach your child that he is perfect without things or entrapments—as he is, without anything attached.

We are not the sum of what we *have*, but rather of what we *are* without anything. The ego should not be tied up in our income but in our deeds. Instead of *give me, get me, buy me,* let's change the message to *teach me, give unconditional love to me, and guide me to respect myself and others.*

Now, that is the best way to indulge your child!

INDEX

ABOUT THE AUTHOR

Donna Corwin has written hundreds of articles on travel, lifestyle, health, and parenting for major magazines such as *Los Angeles Magazine, Parenting, Child, Parents, GQ, Shape, Los Angeles Family, Working Woman, Working Mother, Italian Food & Wine & Travel, Children, Incentive Travel Manager Magazine,* and *The Robb Report.* She was the travel editor and wrote a monthly column, "The Ultimate Itinerary," for Brentwood Media Group magazines including *Beverly Hills 90210, Brentwood News, Santa Monica Sun, Bel-Air View,* and *Malibu Beach* magazines.

Ms. Corwin's work has been featured in dozens of newspapers and articles including *USA Today, The Sacramento Bee, The Denver Post, The Los Angeles Daily News, Woman's World, Publishers Weekly, Colorado Daily News, The Toronto Sun,* and *The Cleveland Plain Dealer.* She was the subject of a feature article in *The Robb Report.*

Ms. Corwin is the author of eight parenting books including the bestselling *TimeOut For Toddlers,* now in its twentieth printing, (Berkley Books, 1992); *Growing Up Great* (Berkley Books, 1994); *The Challenging Child* (Berkley Books, 1996); *The TimeOut Prescription* (Contemporary Books, 1998); *Parent Traps* (St. Martin's Press, 2000); *The Tween Years* (Contemporary Books, 2002); *Pushed To The Edge* (Berkley Books, 2005).

Ms. Corwin has been a spokesperson and parenting expert for Plus Media's Satellite Media and Live Television Tours. She has appeared on over seventy-five national news and morning shows and stations including Fox News, NBC, ABC, CBS, CNN, NewsWatch, and The Daily Buzz. She was also a lifestyle spokesperson for Media Café's Satellite Media Tours. Ms. Corwin has also appeared as a guest expert on numerous television and radio shows including Oprah Winfrey's Oxygen Network, *Rolanda, The Other Half, Home & Family, The Leeza Show, Denver Morning News, Good Morning Utah, Good Day Dallas*, ABC radio, and *The Parents Journal* on

NPR radio. She has been a lecturer on parenting issues for the Motion Picture & Television Fund's Wellness Program and the Educational Records Bureau (ERB) convention. She was a guest speaker in Washington, D.C., for Asset Managers Advisors, speaking on "Surviving the Family Legacy."

She is a member of Writers Guild West and the Screen Actors Guild as well as being cited in *Marquis Who's Who in American Women.*

Ms. Corwin lives in Beverly Hills, California, with her husband, Stan, and their daughter, Alexandra.

Visit Donna Corwin at www.donnacorwin.com.

Spend time with your children

Robyn Spizman and Evelyn Sacks

EAT NAP PLAY

How to Get Even More Out
of Your Child's Day for Less

Code # 3612 • Paperback • $14.95

Stuck at home with bored kids and a nonexistent entertainment budget? House covered with a sea of toys that nobody wants to play with? Looking for ways to raise resilient kids without throwing away your hard-earned cash? **Eat, Nap, Play** is a timely guide that will help smart moms maximize the time they spend with their children without breaking the bank.